"We'd better listen to Brian McLaren if we want to bring the reality of Christ into the world as it is and the church as it now is."
—DALLAS WILLARD, Author, *The Spirit of the Disciplines* and *The Divine Conspiracy*

"This is a book about giving your church a 100,000 mile major tune-up and possible overhaul. While re-visioning is never a painless process, *The Church on the Other Side* makes the process hopeful, purposeful, and doable. It's a commonsense book about a crucial leadership milestone. This is a must-read for any leader in a church that's two months to 200 years old."
—BRAD SMITH, President, Leadership Network

"Brian McLaren sees in this new postmodern world wonderful opportunities for the church to be a voice, to tell a story and to connect with people who feel increasingly disconnected at many levels of life. Church leaders serious about engaging this world will want to read this book and discuss it together."
—MIKE REGELE, Author, *Death of the Church*

"*The Church on the Other Side* keeps away from both jargon and the easy, how-to answers we all know don't work. I highly recommend this book for leaders looking for a clear and concise diagnosis of our challenges and a new map for taking the journey."
—ALAN J. ROXBURGH, Director of Leadership Development, Percept

"Brian McLaren caused me to 'rethink' church. He's relevant, challenging, practical, and a great writer. His high regard for the bride of Christ is evident as he pushes us to redefine and design a stronger church in the 21st century."
—JIM BURNS, Ph.D., President, National Institute of Youth Ministry

"Brian McLaren is fearless in leading the way for *The Church on the Other Side*. Thank God for spiritual frontrunners like Brian who will risk the mapping of postmodern Christianity."
—TODD HUNTER, Former President/National Director, Association of Vineyard Churches

"This is a marvelous book. Brian McLaren proposes bold new strategies in a winsome manner—and with a deep commitment to bringing the unchanging Gospel to our rapidly changing world."
—RICHARD J. MOUW, President and Professor of Christian Philosophy, Fuller Theological Seminary; Author, *The Smell of Sawdust*

Also by Brian McLaren

Finding Faith

More Ready Than You Realize

A Is for Abductive (with Leonard Sweet and Jerry Haselmayer)

The Church on the Other Side

Doing Ministry in the Postmodern Matrix

Brian D. McLaren

REVISED AND EXPANDED EDITION
OF *REINVENTING YOUR CHURCH*

ZONDERVAN™

GRAND RAPIDS, MICHIGAN 49530

ZONDERVAN™

The Church on the Other Side
Copyright © 1998, 2000 by Brian D. McLaren
Formerly titled *Reinventing Your Church*

Requests for information should be addressed to:

Zondervan, *Grand Rapids, Michigan 49530*

Library of Congress Cataloging-in-Publication Data

McLaren, Brian D., 1956–
    The church on the other side : doing ministry in the postmodern matrix
/ Brian D. McLaren.
      p.   cm.
Rev. ed. of: Reinventing your church.
Includes bibliographical references.
    ISBN: 0-310-25219-9 (softcover)
    1.Church renewal.   I. McLaren, Brian D., 1956–   II. Title.
BV600.2 .M37 2000
262'.001'7 — dc21   00–039261

Interior design by Sherri L. Hoffman

Printed in the United States of America

---

05 06 07 08 /❖ DC/ 13 12 11 10 9 8

CONTENTS

*T*he title for the first edition of this book was *Reinventing Your Church* and in this new, expanded edition, we are "reinventing this book." The new title is really more appropriate for a number of reasons.

Reinventing echoed the language of a 1980s church-growth book, and this book is, I hope, more about the 2080s than the 1980s.

Your Church seemed to focus on one individual church, but this book is really about a revolution that will affect, to one degree or another, every church in the world.

Reinventing might sound like the language of engineering, but this book really deals with the church as a love affair, a spiritual romance, a labor of love, a work of faith and art. It sees the church as a community that must be understood and befriended, not just a machine to be tinkered with and tuned up.

Your Church seemed to suggest that the church really is ours. That is misleading in two ways. First, the church isn't ours; it's God's. And second, it isn't ours; it's us. Thus *Reinventing Us* would have been a more accurate title.

Although *The Church on the Other Side* isn't exactly clear (people ask, "What's it about?"), it does have a certain mystique. And that's an accurate reflection about where we are going in this book. We are "exploring off the map"—looking into mysterious territory beyond our familiar world on this side of the river, this side of the ocean, this side of the boundary between modern and postmodern worlds. We are looking into an exciting, unmapped world on the other side of all we know so far.

So, what is the book about? It is about doing ministry on the other side of the modern/postmodern transition.

The word *Matrix* in the subtitle means a place or environment within which something originates, emerges, takes form, or develops. The church that took form in the medieval matrix differed substantially from the church in the ancient matrix; the church that emerged in the modern matrix likewise differed from the church in the medieval matrix. The question for us is how the church will emerge, take form, and develop in the postmodern matrix. And if I am right, this isn't just something we think or read about; this is something we can participate in. I hope you share my excitement (and sense of responsibility) about that. What a time to be alive!

The words *Doing Ministry* in the subtitle suggest the practical focus of this book. Now, I don't want to give all of you pragmatic practitioners the wrong impression: I am more interested in stretching your thinking here than tweaking your techniques, so what you learn here won't be easily boiled down into new tricks you can try this Sunday. In the same way, I must similarly advise all you thinkers and academics: I am a practitioner, not an academic (although I used be a college teacher). As a "practicing pastor" I am rooted in the everyday and down-to-earth tasks of giving sermons, causing and resolving conflicts, answering phone calls and emails about who's singing what in the second service this Sunday, performing weddings and funerals, and that sort of thing. I guess you could say I am a reflective practitioner ... focused on the down-and-dirty of doing ministry, but trying to have a high-altitude understanding of when, where, how, and why we are doing it.

Here is what I believe, and hope:

I believe that thousands of churches are going to find themselves asking questions about the postmodern transition in the next few decades. What is it? What do we do about it? Is it as horrific and evil as the radio preachers make it sound? Does it present opportunity along with challenge? Could the postmodern world be an improvement over the modern, ministry-wise? How will we change if we go with the transition (as opposed to resisting it, isolating from it, denying it)? Does the concept of the postmodern transition help make sense of our chaotic experience as committed Christians over the last few decades?

I hope that this book will be one of the first ones people reach for when they start asking those questions. I hope they will find it clear, honest, open-minded, fun to read, intellectually and spiritually stretching, ecumenical, and solidly rooted in Scripture, real-life church experience, and evangelical ministry. But I hope it won't be the last book they read on the subject. I hope it will instill in readers a desire to continue the conversation by engaging with the thinking of many others who have so much to offer that I cannot. We are all in this together.

Much of the book remains as it appeared in the first edition. However, in addition to smoothing out a few sentences, adding some fine touches here and there, and a few proofreading corrections, there are two more substantive changes.

- The earlier "Strategy 2: Redefine Your Mission" suffered, I think, from an excessively individual focus. I have reworked that chapter with insights on community that I gained from the writings of Lesslie Newbigin and the Gospel and Our Culture Network, whose thinking was far ahead of my own when I originally wrote that chapter in 1996.
- This new version includes an important new chapter on postmodernity. It comes under Strategy 12, as "12.C: Get Ready for Revolution."

I hope that anyone who bought *Reinventing Your Church* and now buys *The Church on the Other Side* will feel that these changes were well worth the price of buying the book again.

I want to thank the scores of people who responded to the first edition with deeply encouraging feedback. I received scores of emails, phone calls, and letters from people who told me the book helped them in many ways. Many told me that their whole church leadership teams read and discussed the book. Many told me it gave them a fresh start in ministry; it renewed their hope that there could be better days ahead "on the other side." Many told me that they hadn't read a book that made them think as many new thoughts as this one, and others told me that it put into words things they were already thinking but hadn't quite wrestled into words. Many told me that they felt relieved ("I'm not crazy after all!") to find someone else saying (finally) what they felt they had been the only ones saying for years. (Others said they still thought they were crazy but were glad to have company in their craziness.) And quite a few said the book helped them help others in new and better ways through their churches and other ministries. All this has been very encouraging and humbling for me to hear. In its new form, I hope God will use this book to do even more. If that happens, I know I will be thanking God, under whose guidance the church emerges and develops from one matrix to the next.

At the same time, I'm aware of how this book raises more questions than it answers, and how it cannot succeed in making the chaos of transitional times feel easy, clear, or safe. I hope you will read it, not as a full solution, but as a small contribution to a much larger conversation and shared initiative. And I hope it will invite and encourage you to contribute as well, because your unique perspectives, experiences, gifts, and resources are needed —now more than ever.

I would like to dedicate this revised/reinvented edition to the people of Cedar Ridge Community Church, who have taken as their vision to become "a dynamic hub of Christian thought, action, community, and creative arts, dedicated to embracing and transforming our postmodern world with the message and love of Jesus Christ." It is an honor to serve with you!

BRIAN MCLAREN
SPENCERVILLE, MARYLAND

INTRODUCTION

If you have a new world,
you need a new church.
You have a new world.

*A*friend of mine just returned from China. He
summed up his experience with this scene: a busy
city, bustling cars, whirring bicycle wheels. Slowly
down the street rumbles a single oxcart full of produce,
led by an old man in a standard navyblue cotton jacket.
The man reaches into his jacket and pulls out . . . a cellular phone. In that one gesture my friend saw our
modern world, from oxcarts to bicycles to automobiles,
swept away by a whole new age.

Under our feet, the earth is moving. I am not speaking of the normal yearly rotation or daily revolution of
the earth, as dramatic as both are. I am speaking of an
even more dramatic, historic, unrepeatable kind of
movement. We don't feel it, at least not in everyday living. But scientists have proved that our continents rest
on large, fractured plates of the earth's crust. These
plates slide around on a plastic interior, jostling, grinding, some riding up on others, some being thrust under.
At the edges, where two plates meet, we occasionally get
clues as to the enormous pressures that routinely strain
the earth beneath our feet day by day. At those edges, at
those occasional moments of crisis, the movement is visible and even frightening. We get earthquakes.

In earthquakes, pressures build to a point at which
plates fracture or rise or fall or slip—and at the edges,
we can feel the shake. Afterward, another period of
apparent calm returns—for a while.

Human history seems to behave like the earth. There are predictable, repeating cycles not unlike the earth's rotation. There are also unpredictable processes—usually subtle, occasionally dramatic. We can live for years quite unaware of how pressures are building, but then, seemingly out of nowhere, tremors start to occur with increasing frequency. Sometimes we encounter a "big one," and almost overnight our world changes so dramatically that old maps no longer fit the new reality.

OLD MAPS, NEW WORLD

You and I happen to have been born at an "edge," at a time of high "tectonic activity" in history—the end of one age and the beginning of another. It is a time of shaking. Yesterday's maps are already outdated, and today's soon will be, too. The uncharted world ahead of us is what we will call "the new world on the other side": the other side of two world wars and one cold war, the other side of communism, the other side of theological liberalism, the other side of the second millennium, the other side of modernism. There used to be an Old World, then a New World, then the Third World, but now all three are being swept up in a *new* new world.

Or on a slightly grander scale, there used to be a prehistoric world, an ancient world, a medieval world, and a modern world, but now all four are being swept up in a *postmodern* world.

During the last hundred years, and especially the last fifty, old-world technology has intensified cultural pressures and unleashed tremor after tremor, each far more significant than could ever have been imagined. These technological tremors have helped bring to an end the old world that created them. Think of the automobile and its effects on the environment, the economy, the family unit, and even courtship and sexuality (especially when the car is equipped with a back seat). Think of radio, air travel, birth-control pills, antibiotics, and the cathode ray tube—and we're barely past the midcentury mark. Then came the tidal wave of social change set in motion during the sixties. No wonder the old maps don't fit the new world!

Think of space travel and the personal computer, the cellular phone and the microwave, the fax machine and the Internet, the compact disc and genetic engineering. (I heard Dr. Leonard Sweet of Drew University say that the most significant scientific milestone of the whole Twentieth century may have occurred in 1995, as the human genome project reached the 50 percent point in mapping the human gene. Five years later, the preliminary map was completed. Who knows where that will lead—what horrors, what wonders?)

It is as if during our lifetime, plate tectonics went into fast forward—as if, before our eyes, Africa and South America separated, Australia migrated from southeastern India, and ice caps melted so the seas would rise. Who will draw maps to trace the new world reforming around us? What will this new world be like, we wonder?

No, I am not one who has idealistic notions of a millennial "new world order." The new world on the other side will have the same old problems—a stubborn human nature, ecological risks, economic pain, hunger, disease, racism, sexism, *all* kinds of sin. But these problems must be faced in a new way because—make no mistake—a new world is bursting forth beneath our bands of concrete and asphalt, erupting under our miles of wire drooping between creosoted telephone poles, heaving its strength like tectonic plates to crack presumably solid foundations.

If you are a Christian of any sort—liberal, conservative, evangelical, mainline, Catholic, Protestant, hand-clapper, nonclapper, devotee of pipe organ or keyboard, of piano or guitar—or even if you are not a Christian, you recognize that these grinding, shifting, transitional times have shaken the church. It is unsettled, imbalanced, nervous, reeling, sometimes oblivious but more often these days wide-eyed and openmouthed with speechless anxiety, wondering when the shaking will be over. Is the church a dinosaur at the end of the Jurassic? Will it survive the changes?

NO RELIGION? NOT AN OPTION

Also, Christian or not, you are aware of Western culture's spiritual vacuum, of its deepening sighs for a life of the spirit. This need will only intensify on the other side. If the late old world taught us anything, it is this: Human beings are indeed incurably religious, and we—as individuals, as groups, as a civilization— need a spiritual resource.

For a variety of reasons, organized religion, including Christianity, seemed to have lost its power to satisfy us in the late old world. It seemed ingrown, tired, petty, crotchety, and out of touch—or else manic, wild-eyed, and lunatic. As a result, many of us disengaged from religion. But we eventually learned—from totalitarian materialism on both sides of the Iron Curtain—that there is no alternative: If we cannot find good religion, and cannot do without, we will turn to bad religion.

Even an agnostic or an atheist, then, can see the need for new kinds of churches in the new world—churches that once again replenish the spiritually hungry and thirsty, that understand them and connect them with the mysteries they seek; churches that promote a healthful, whole, hearty spirituality rather than an ugly, thin, hateful, insipid, or anemic religion. Which churches will meet this need? Who will design, build, lead, join, support, and encourage them? Where will you and I fit in?

SECOND THOUGHTS?

Right about now, some of us are wishing we could go back to the old world. We love our old maps and wish the world still matched them. But others of us are eager to explore the new world, to create new maps, to learn the new lay of the land, to make the world on the other side a good world, and to make a positive difference in it. How can we serve wisely and well in the settlement of the new world? Many of us believe that the revitalization and reconfiguration of the Christian church is the best strategy possible.

You see, if we have a new world, we will need a new church. We won't need a new religion per se, but a new framework for our theology. Not a new Spirit, but a new spirituality. Not a new Christ, but a new Christian. Not a new denomination, but a new kind of church in every denomination. Yet we should not underestimate either side of the equation—what must change as well as what must not.

Someone has said that the learners will inherit the earth while the learned are equipped to face a world that no longer exists. That's the reality of the new world. Actually, there may no longer be such a thing as the learned in the new world—only learners and nonlearners. And if only the fittest survive, then perhaps we're being too optimistic. Maybe there will be no nonlearners—only fast learners who thrive and slow learners who merely survive.

I like the new world that I see so far. It drives me crazy sometimes, but I am optimistic. I wouldn't want to go back to the old world. Perhaps I am just tired of it. The new world seems to be filled with opportunity—or maybe I am just being naïve and don't see that disaster lurks around the bend. We will eventually find out. Lyle Schaller is probably most realistic when he suggests that the "different world" we face today and tomorrow has both opportunities and price tags: "Different often is better. . . . Everything in life, except grace, has a price tag."[1]

So here we are, in a transition zone of high tectonic activity, on the threshold of a new world, in a time when many old churches are being shaken half to death, barely surviving, too rarely thriving. And where they are thriving, it's for one of two reasons: Either they are creating time warps where the past will be preserved so reactionary folk can flock there for a safe—temporary—old familiar haven; or they are among the learners at the top who are surfing change into the new world and transitioning old churches of yesterday into the new churches of the other side.

The point is, if you have a new world, you need a new church. You have a new world.

This book is for people who don't think we can go back to the old world—and don't want to. It is for people who want to help define and shape the church of the future, under the guidance of God. It is a proposal for strategies for making the transition to the church that will be.

This is not a formulaic how-to book. It's not about seven easy steps to anything. It's not about how I or the people of my congregation figured out THE SECRET and how YOU CAN TOO! Rather, this is a book about the hard work of fresh thinking—innovative, bold, creative thinking. That doesn't mean this book is impractical, because sometimes the most practical thing we can do is stop and think, especially when we are encountering something fresh and different.

Ken Blanchard talks about four levels of change.[2] The easiest change to effect is growth in knowledge: We teach others, they gain knowledge, and change has occurred. The second change, attitude, with its emotional component, is much tougher to deal with. Third and still more difficult is behavioral change—overcoming habits and replacing old patterns with new. Fourth and most difficult of all is organizational change, a process that takes time, energy, sweat, and often blood and tears, too.

In this book we are dealing with a fifth level of change—a kind of change that requires the other four levels to happen at the same time. It is no wonder that we need some strategies to help us cope with this change and guide us through it.

In 1970, Francis Schaeffer saw the change coming:

> The church today should be getting ready and talking about issues of tomorrow and not issues of 20 and 30 years ago, because the church is going to be squeezed in a wringer. If we found it tough in these last few years, what are we going to do when we are faced with the real changes that are ahead? . . .
>
> One of the greatest injustices we do to our young people is to ask them to be conservative. Christianity is not conservative, but revolutionary. To be conservative today is to miss the whole point, for conservatism means standing in the flow of the status quo, and the status quo no longer belongs to us. . . .
>
> If we want to be fair, we must teach the young to be revolutionaries, revolutionaries against the status quo.[3]

I was in college when I first read those words. Now, over the threshhold of the twenty-first century, with my own kids in college, Schaeffer's words about revolution feel even more poignant, more stirring. I want to give my children a faith intended for revolution, not for status quo. And not just my children. I want that for myself—and for you.

You can read these strategies in any order. You may accept some and reject others. You should plan to add to the list, because what you will find here is surely not the last word. As incomplete and imperfect though these proposed strategies may be, God willing, they will get many of us thinking together and working together in what may be the most important, most revolutionary task of our generation—planting and developing the church on the other side.

Maximize Discontinuity

Distinguish between
renewed, restored, and
reinvented churches, and
focus on the last.

*H*ere we are, in this middle zone, this transition zone. Behind us is the old world, and on the other side of our middle zone is the new world. We are struggling like swimmers in a crosscurrent, trying to figure out how to get out of these frightening waves and make some headway, wondering if we'll make it. Some are trying to tell us the currents aren't so bad, that we will be okay if we just hold steady; soon everything will be as it was before if we just hang in there, resist the change, and go back. It is comforting advice and appeals to many—but I think it is fatal.

That is why our first strategy is to maximize discontinuity. That is to say, maybe small changes, superficial changes, were enough in the past. But the degree of change we are experiencing now is such that small measures, even a lot of them, aren't enough. Instead, we need major change, qualitative change, revolution, rebirth, reinvention, and not just once, but repeatedly for the foreseeable future.

Margaret Wheatley, in her inspiring book *Leadership and the New Science*, tells a story of the famous physicists Niels Bohr and Werner Heisenburg. In the early twentieth century, they faced a situation analogous in many ways to ours: Their theories didn't fit their newest data. Heisenburg recalled the emotional upheaval of that time:

> I remember discussions with Bohr which went through many hours till very late at night and ended almost in despair; and when at the end of

the discussion I went alone for a walk in the neighboring park
I repeated to myself again and again the question: Can nature
possibly be so absurd as it seemed to us in these atomic
experiments? . . . here the foundations of physics have started
moving; and . . . this motion has caused the feeling that the
ground would be cut from science.

From that frustration, as the old Newtonian paradigm proved
inadequate to cope with subatomic reality, a breakthrough
occurred and quantum theory was born.[1]

For us, the upheaval is equally intense. Our theology, our ways
of doing ministry, don't seem to work or fit anymore. We have
long discussions, take long walks, and ask agonizing questions, but
can't see yet that a breakthrough may just be around the corner,
opening the way to exciting new discoveries. We need hope.

If we could get even a brief and dim sighting of where we're
going, of what life and faith will be like on the other side of this
frustration, I think we would gain new hope. Because as frightening as these crosscurrents may be, we will see that on the other side
is, as the children of Israel discovered, "a good land, flowing with
milk and honey." If we can get a vision of what the land on the other
side is like, we can help others make the crossing, too. It all starts
with a glimpse, a sighting, a shout: "There it is, over there! That's
where we need to go!"

Many gifted leaders and wise writers are helping us get the
needed sightings. They are painting vivid and inspiring pictures
for us: the rediscovered, seeker-driven church (Bill Hybels), the
purpose-driven church (Rick Warren), the permission-giving
church (William Easum), the resurrected church (Mike Regele),
the twenty-first century church (Leith Anderson), the metamor-
phosed church (Carl George), the new apostolic church (George
Hunter), the missional church (Alan Roxburgh and others) and
more. And on this they nearly all seem to agree: The future
belongs to those willing to let go, to stop trying to minimize the
change we face, but rather to maximize the discontinuity. William
Easum writes,

A new form of congregational life is dragging Christians kicking and screaming into the twenty-first century. The self-understanding, focus, corporate culture, leadership, organizational styles, and strategies are radically different from those experienced throughout the twentieth century. The future church offers new opportunities and problems and requires a new mindset. . . .

We live in a time unlike any other time that any living person has known. It's not merely that things are changing. Change itself has changed, thereby changing the rules by which we live. . . . [T]here is more to this change than simply a linear extrapolation of rapid change and complexity. Quantum leaps are happening that are nothing like evolution. They remove us almost totally from our previous context. Simply learning to do old chores faster or to be able to adapt old forms to more complex situations no longer produces the desired results. . . . Running harder and harder in ministry will not work in this new world. . . .

Established churches are becoming increasingly ineffective because our past has not prepared us for ministry in the future. The discontinuity we have experienced because of these quantum leaps is comparable to the experience of the residents of East Berlin when the Berlin Wall came down. Nothing in their past prepared them for life without the Wall. Very little in our past has prepared us for ministry in today's world."[2]

To maximize discontinuity, it helps to distinguish between three kinds of churches: new, renewed, and restored.

As we shall see, it is possible to have a new church that is *not* a new church, and an old church that *is* a new church. *New,* as we will use the term here, means new in kind, not in age. A new church is one designed for the future, reinvented and reintroduced for the other side. It is an evolving organism at the beginning (or end) of an ice age, capable of adjusting to the coming climatic and environmental upheavals. But the new, reinvented church—the church on the other side—must be distinguished from two other subspecies in the church genus: the renewed church and the restored church.

THE RENEWED CHURCH

The renewed church is an old church that, after having lost touch with its own people, goes through a process of change in order to relate to them and better meet their needs again. This is good. But renewal tends to be a temporary, or stopgap, measure. For example, let's say a church in 2009 is functioning with an 1889 style. Its members, trying to negotiate between their church world and their contemporary world, are themselves, on average, 1959-style people. The church is thus 120 years behind the surrounding culture and 70 years behind its own subculture. Renewal means it catches up to, say, 1989. This is traumatic—a huge change after generations of no change!

Three problems remain, however, even after renewal. First, the leadership of the church is now thirty years ahead of the people, who therefore become uneasy: Are we compromising with "the world"? Are we losing our "salt"? Are we pandering to the fads of the fickle masses? Second, in spite of everything, the leadership is still twenty years behind the times, so a spiritual seeker walking through the doors still feels he or she has entered a time warp and can't tell whether God is outdated and out of touch or just this church. Third, twenty years from now, the renewed church will be back in trouble again—forty years behind the surrounding culture, and some years behind its own subculture.

By contrast, the new church not only changes its style, but it changes its attitude. Change is accepted as an unchanging fact of life. The new church not only catches up to the present but also corrects those tendencies that would make it keep falling behind. It removes the antichange bias.

THE RESTORED CHURCH

The restored church looks at problems in the churches today and says, "Aha! We've lost our way! We must go back to the New Testament to rediscover our original vibrancy." This is an intelligent realization. Unfortunately, what tends to happen next is that we latch onto some peripheral matter of early church life and prescribe it as the missing feature. It's what my friend Peter Morris calls the Last Detail, or the Lost Detail—the thing that will make all the difference once it is restored: "speaking in tongues!" "the five-fold ministry of apostles, prophets, evangelists, pastors, and teachers!" "a love feast!" "foot-washing!" "no church buildings!" "no paid pastors!" "a plurality of elders!" "spontaneous, non-planned meetings!" "one church per city!" "healings!" "communal living!"

Inevitably, after being seized upon as "the secret," this lost detail assumes a significance far beyond all sane proportions. Eventually, maintaining and celebrating this distinctive detail becomes the church's raison d'être. After all, it's what makes "us" special.

"The Church of the Lost Detail" approach has been tried so many times as to make a middle-aged man cynical, but it holds great appeal for young revolutionaries, cranks, and folk of a romantic bent.

But the church on the other side has little in common with all this. The new church sees problems of struggling older churches and, instead of becoming judgmental ("They've compromised! They're no longer biblical!"), becomes sympathetic ("They're doing their best, but the world is changing so fast, and a thousand sociological forces work against rapid enough adaptation.")

The new church does not view the New Testament as a "New Leviticus"—a law book of strict rules—nor as a fixed, detailed blueprint to be applied to all churches in all cultures across time. Rather, the New Testament serves as (among other things) an inspired, exemplary, and eternally relevant case study of how the early church itself adapted and evolved and coped with rapid change and new challenges. In place of a fixed structure that is to fit all, the new church advocates a flexible, adaptable, evolving structure that is developed to meet the current needs. The key word is adaptability.

As a result, the new church never expects to "get it right." It doesn't expect to finally find the magic pattern or resurrect the lost, last detail that will suddenly spell supernatural success for the body of Christ. It assumes that as long as the church grows, it will have to adapt and change and learn. As long as there are people, there will be problems; as long as there is history, there will be struggle; as long as the church exists in this troubled world, it will compete neck and neck against the gates of hell to see who will prevail against whom. As long as we keep having children, those offspring will eventually rise up and call us outdated.

The new church makes these assumptions because this adaptability is just what biblical history illustrates.

So the new church should be distinguished from both renewed and restored churches.

THE REINVENTED CHURCH

The new church can be of any age, any denomination. It goes through a process of peripheral change similar to the renewed and restored churches, a process of radical self-assessment, of going back to roots, sources, and first things. But the new church does not try to draft a new blueprint. Instead, it comes up with a new philosophy of ministry that prepares it to meet whatever unforeseen changes are to come. To use contemporary jargon, it discovers "new paradigms." In biblical terms, it seeks not only new wineskins (renewal), but new wine—which includes a new attitude toward wineskins in general. The church decides that it loves new wine so much, it will never again be so attached to wineskins of any sort. Then, when the wineskins need to be discarded, they can be with a minimum of anguish. When an old church thus reinvents itself, it is born again as a new church, like a caterpillar entering its cocoon and emerging as a butterfly. In so doing, the church has maximized discontinuity.

I like the way Leadership Network's *NetFax* put it:[3]

> Paradigm pliancy is the best strategy in times of rapid and turbulent change. Flexibility and a willingness to abandon outmoded methods and approaches is crucial. When the horse is dead, dismount.

Maximizing continuity means not trying to fix up the horse to get a few more miles out of it, but burying it and looking for a new one. The journey is the important thing, not the horse you take to get there.

STRATEGY ONE

This won't be an easy journey even after we have dismounted from the old dead horse. That's why it is worth this investment of time, thought, dialogue, prayer, and preparation. If we agree on this first strategy—that the future requires maximizing discontinuity by aiming for new, reconceived, or reinvented churches rather than renewed or restored ones—then we have already made important progress, and we're ready to move on.

Think of it like this: Imagine that your church has to go through 150 changes over the next five years to get from where it is to where it needs to be. Imagine fighting 150 battles, one at a time, each one more difficult than the last because people's change-fatigue and change-aversion intensify with each change. No one would survive this five years' war! Now imagine: If it took you four and a half of your five years to bring about just one change—just one profound, elegant, simple (but difficult, make no mistake) change, namely, a change in your church's attitude toward change—wouldn't that make the other 149 changes more feasible? That is what I mean by maximizing discontinuity: Change your church's attitude toward change, and everything else will change as it should. That one change has leverage to make possible all the rest. Without that one radical discontinuity—even though it seems hard, so hard —the other changes are impossible, so impossible.

I know something about discontinuity. This isn't just theory for me. With the help of our good friends Bill and Shobha Duncan, my wife and I planted a church in 1982. By 1985 I was becoming disillusioned. Although our little church had grown from eleven people to about a hundred, nearly all of the people attending had come to us from other churches. I began attending seminars led by megachurch pastors, especially those touting a "seeker sensitivity" approach. I became more and more convinced that they were on the right track. So I did what thousands of other pastors did in the eighties and early nineties—I tried to put into practice what I learned at the seminars. But like thousands of other pastors, I had to admit a couple of years later that I had spilled a lot of blood (that's barely a hyperbole) with little to show for it.

In late 1987, I approached the Leadership Team at my church and said something like this: "We're working hard, and we're a happy church, but we're drawing all our people from the minority who are already churchgoers. We have seen very few conversions from the secular majority. That means that although we have a nice warm church, we are out of touch with the very people whom Jesus came to seek and save. We've tried to remedy this through a series of hard-won changes, but so far, nothing has really clicked. So I have a proposal...."

What followed was a radical—for us—proposal for maximizing discontinuity. Instead of continually making gradual changes—as in music and service format—in hopes that their cumulative effect would make us more effective, I suggested we make an abrupt, discontinuous change. I said something like this: "I propose that we go to the church and tell them we would like to disband. At the same time, we invite them to become part of a church planting team to launch a new church ten months from now. Then we'd spend the next ten months in a gestation period, an incubation period, going back to ground zero to come up with a new mission statement and a strategy that we think will work at reaching nonchurch people. We'd train our people to become the core of a whole new kind of church."

The Leadership Team accepted the proposal. Together we led our church through a ten-month gestation period. We moved to a new location, took on a new name, and developed a whole new philosophy of ministry. No, our story isn't nearly as dramatic or outstanding as that of Willow Creek or Saddleback Community Church, but that core of eighty people who went with us soon tripled in size—and nearly all the new people were from the secular majority. I wouldn't have known what to call it back then, but today I would say that,with God's help, we maximized discontinuity. Thus began my experience with the church on the other side.

Redefine Your Mission

*Clarify and simplify to
"more Christians, better
Christians" in authentic
missional community,
for the good of the world.*

*T*he church has acted in different ways in history, depending on what was required of it—or what it was tricked into—according to the times. For example, on occasion the church has hunted down and killed heretics, while on occasion it itself has been vilified as a heretical organization. It has sometimes opposed the progress of science but sometimes has vigorously promoted progress. The church has preserved ancient culture and dead languages, eradicated ancient cultures and languages, fostered great art, fostered tacky art, destroyed great art, launched and supported missionary expansion, ridiculed and hindered missionary expansion, healed the sick and fed the hungry, ignored the sick and forgotten the hungry, inspired capitalistic achievement, critiqued capitalistic achievement, opposed communism, baptized communism, promoted conservative politics, promoted liberal politics, fought other denominations, promoted ecumenism, retreated into a subculture, penetrated new cultures. . . .

Sometimes the church has found itself doing opposite things at the same time. That's how life goes, and no doubt, that won't change on the other side. More surprising, though, is this: For a lot of the time, much of the Christian church didn't seem to ask itself what its mission is, or whether it even has one. It seemed to just go along without any internal gyroscope or hard drive moving it out from the inside.

I believe this befuddlement about mission must change on the other side. The new church must define—or redefine—its mission. The specific focus of local churches will vary, of course, according to their context and environment. But I believe four overriding values will move to the forefront of the new church's mission:

1. More Christians
2. Better Christians
3. Authentic missional community
4. For the good of the world

WHICH COMES FIRST?

*T*he four tasks obviously go together, but in which order? Some may argue that the one listed second should come first. Why? Because the new Christians who are won from the secular and nominally religious majority will need to be mentored by existing Christians. If the students become like their teachers, we will run the risk of ending up with more mediocre Christians unless we first attend to improving the prototypes. So we will need *better* before we go for *more*. In addition, non-Christians will not want to become Christians unless there are more credible Christians and Christian communities for them to observe. Chuck Colson argues this point well:

> Alasdair MacIntyre observes in *Difficulties in Christian Belief* that ... "Where the Christian community is incapable of producing lives such as those of the saints, the premises from which it argues will appear rootless and arbitrary." But a Christian community that produces love and beauty is a witness that cannot be denied. ... We must first be people who live out the gospel. [Stanley] Hauerwas writes, God's truth is credible to the world only when it sees a community shaped by the truth. ... If the gospel is to be heard, it must also be seen.[1]

Of course, the reverse could also be argued: that the task of improving existing Christians (crotchety and stubborn as we are) is more daunting than the task of building a new generation of better Christians from scratch. Thus the fastest way to *better* is by focusing first on the *more*. Lyle Schaller's pithy dictum suggests as much: "Bring in a new day with new people."

Or perhaps there aren't really two tasks at all. Or perhaps it's wrongheaded to have the two compete for priority, as if pulse and brainwaves were competitors for survival. The fact is, if we are truly building better Christians, they will be concerned about evangelism, yielding more; if we really expect to succeed at evangelism, we know we must also face the task of discipleship producing better. So perhaps we would do better, on the other side, to take both tasks and subsume them under the single heading "Disciple Making." Whatever terminology we use, we need to face the fact that we are not doing well enough on either account at present.

Consider this. When I originally wrote this chapter, the world was still feeling the shock of an unimaginable genocide in Rwanda, Africa. I could have boarded a plane to Rwanda and found villages where dried human corpses were still strewn on streets, crumpled under church pews, rotting in fields, full of bullets, too many to bury. Think about the magazine cover pictures or evening news shots you have seen. (The latter might as well all be still photos, since nothing moves except flies.) The untold part of the story is this: Rwanda was arguably the most Christianized country in Africa. Both tribes who engaged in mutual attempted genocide were predominantly Christian, at least in name. Rwanda has often been cited as a shining success story of evangelical missions.

WHAT'S WRONG WITH THIS PICTURE?

I see all of us Christians reflected in our Rwandan brothers and sisters. Something is wrong with us, our discipleship, our faith. If "we"—not just we humans, but specifically we humans called Christians—can kill each other in Rwanda, don't you agree something is wrong with us? Closer to home, if those who call themselves Christians can engage in sexual scandalfests, conduct racial cold wars in America, kill Muslims in Bosnia, and hate each other in Ireland, doesn't something have to change?

I can't shake my head at the Rwandans, the televangelists, the Bosnians, or anyone else who appears to "do things I wouldn't do," because I'm not sure I'm all that different. All of us who take the name "Christian" claim a faith that is supposed to unleash spiritual power in us, but the darker powers of hate and fear (not to mention lust and greed) seem stronger. I see my own country—also among the most "Christian" in the world—born through the near extermination of one race, reared on the subjugation of another race, and enriched through the rape of one of the finest environments on the planet, as Jim Wallis of Sojourners poignantly suggests. Where was our faith? Why was it not potent enough to help us see what we were doing?

As I look around today, sin seems stronger than God the Father sometimes, sex stronger than Jesus, money stronger than the Holy Spirit, propaganda stronger than the gospel. This contradicts my faith, and so I am at a loss, wanting neither to hide from the facts nor to jettison the faith. The most upstanding Christians of the new church on the other side may not, I think, be much better than the Christians of the old church, although some improvement would be nice, please God. But the Christians of the new church will, I hope, at least be honest about the failure of our Christian faith to make us much better. That in itself will, perhaps, be a small improvement.

When I say "our" Christian faith in this context I mean, of course, our version of it. As C. S. Lewis said, it's useful to distinguish "our religion" from the Christian faith: "Each of us has his individual emphasis: each holds, in addition to the Faith, many opinions which seem to him to be consistent with it and true and important. . . . we are defending Christianity, not 'my religion.'"[2]

POWER DEFICIT

My critique is not of the Faith, but of our version of it. We, with "our" faith, have lost our saltiness, and so, our Lord said, we are fit for nothing and should be thrown out, to be trampled under foot by men (Matthew 5:13). And to a degree, we have been trampled. We complain about this and moan that secular humanists and "the liberal media" are making us victims and treating us unfairly—but fail to realize that our lack of respect merely affirms the truth of Jesus Christ's words! We deserve to be trampled when we claim a faith of such power and show so little of it in our lives.

(Yes, I am aware of "power evangelism," "power encounters," "laughing revivals," and the rest. They have their place, but isn't the power we really long to see not just a matter of shaking a person's limbs or emotions or vocal apparatus but rather the power to shake our selfishness, pettiness, prejudice, laziness, and fear? I am waiting for a power encounter that results not just in tongues-speaking but in sustained tithing, not just in hankering for physical healing but in sustained effort for racial healing, not just in emotional manifestations but in better art and better ecology and more neighborly people. That would be miraculous enough for me at this point.)

The new church must face this power deficit and be serious about building better Christians out of us all. So what would a better Christian look like? What is the profile of the new Christian? This is something for every pastor and serious Christian in this transition zone to lie awake at night struggling with and praying about. Whatever the profile is, it must be realistic; the last thing we need is to create some ideal that will either make us all feel more guilty than we already do, or make us all look like even bigger fools when we fail to live up to our new, higher ideal. That's something I love about the Gospels: We see Jesus calling the disciples to a better way, yet we see them as quite normal buffoons like the rest of us, bumbling along toward it. The Bible has realism.

But the Bible also maintains an idealism—the ideal that people can be "born again." People can grow toward the kind of straight-talking, enemy-loving, phariseeism-transcending, skeptic-inspiring, poor-in-spirit, and rich-in-Spirit discipleship our Lord proclaimed. Jesus can turn a ragtag band of fishermen, rednecks, intellectuals, and common folk into a community of difference-makers. He can start with raw material such as we are.

RAW MATERIAL

*T*his is the other part of the new church mission. The church on the other side must increasingly begin with "rawer" raw material. The goal is not just to turn a nominal Catholic into a back-slapping Baptist, or a backwoods Pentecostal into a refined Episcopalian, or a constipated Presbyterian into an extroverted charismatic. No, not for the new church. There the challenge will be to turn a secular atheist (or a secular nominalist for that matter) into an enthusiastic student of the wisdom and ways of Jesus Christ. The challenge will be to take a young woman who has been abused by her incestuous father and brothers and help her regain her sanity and learn to laugh again—with the laughter of God. The challenge will be to take a right-wing Republican and teach him a love that bonds him to the left-wing Democrat (or whatever either party's descendants will be called as the new world unfolds). The challenge will be to take good middle-class dentists and accountants and help them emerge from their suburban cocoons to care for their neighbors, including their unwashed blue-collar or urban-refugee neighbors, in Jesus' name. The challenge will be to get black folk who resent whites and white folk who resent blacks to come together as brothers and sisters who see their humble, barrier-bridging friendships as a form of quiet, powerful revolution.

In the new church, then, we must start with people in all their rawness—MTV addicts, New Agers, divorcees, substance abusers, intellectual skeptics, semi-literate street people, radio talk-show callers, even radio talk-show hosts—and offer them the hope of becoming, as new Christians, agents of the new church in the new world on the other side.

This new attitude towards "raw" people is already emerging. In recent years the buzzword for this approach has been "seeker sensitivity." This is a good term, though perhaps, as with all jargon, we get sick of it after a while. This concept is a key to the mission of the new church, because the old church had become increasingly seeker-hostile. And it wasn't just the music. Anachronistic music was the least serious, the most superficial—and the most obvious—

of the church's problems. Let me touch briefly on a few of the deeper attitudinal issues.

SEEKER HOSTILITY

*F*or starters, somehow we Christians, especially evangelicals, convinced ourselves of the myth that America used to be a Christian nation—"our" nation—and some bad people took it away from us. Let me just ask: When was it a Christian nation? When we were killing, culturally imprisoning, and stealing the lands of millions of native peoples in a New World version of the holocaust? When we were importing and exploiting millions of slaves? I believe the Christian nation myth is untrue, but more than that, it is pernicious for what it does to us.

The myth turns us into victims (Those bad guys took away our country!), aggressors (We're going to take it back, so watch out!), and defenders (Quick! Circle the wagons!). As aggressive, defensive victims, we hardly carry the posture of Jesus Christ, who came to seek and to save the lost, who had compassion on the nameless crowds. As aggressive, defensive victims, we sound more and more like the Pharisees, who said, "This cursed mob doesn't know God's Word!" (see John 7:49), and less and less like Jesus, who said, "These poor people are harassed and helpless, like sheep without a shepherd" (see Matthew 9:36). The cover story of the November 1995 issue of *Moody Monthly* described the problem too well: "Sinners in the Hands of Angry Christians."

In the new church, this attitude toward non-Christians will change. "The world" will be viewed less and less as the bad boys out there whom we fear, fight, and resist, whom we seek to control through legislation and intimidation with a self-righteous sense of superiority. Instead, "the world" will be viewed more and more as the needy neighbors who haven't yet found the grace that has found us, who receive our love because God loved them enough to send his Son to give them eternal life (John 3:16), who are doing the best they can with what they've got, and who can't be expected to do any better until we find ways to help them want what we've got. (The real test will be whether we can have this attitude even if we are persecuted violently in the world on the other side, as we may be.)

ONE NEGLECTED DETAIL

*I*n all our talk about seeker-sensitive churches and services, I fear we have neglected one small detail: seeker-sensitive Christians. Christians in the new church must really love non-Christians. They must see their mission as helping these uncommitted people become, not "twice as much a son of hell" as we are (see Matthew 23:15), but vibrant followers of Jesus Christ instead.

This is instant oatmeal to say, and brain surgery to do, of course. But even this simple articulation of our mission of disciple-making— more Christians, better Christians—is still incomplete.

I had to make a humbling admission as I prepared the corrections for the new edition of this book. In its original form I had said that our mission on the other side will consist of just two elements (more Christians, better Christians) and I had left out the third and fourth elements (authentic community, for the good of the world) entirely. Why had I left them out? Because even though I was writing a book on the modern/postmodern transition, and even though I was being asked to speak all over the country on the subject, in this very important area I was still quite bound by a very modern and truncated understanding of mission.

MY FIRST MISSION OMISSION

*M*y first run at this chapter implied that God, like any good modern, is interested only in individuals. In the church on the other side we will have to celebrate again the biblical vision of reality, namely, that when God sees his creation, he sees (along with individuals) the unifying, inclusive realities of the group, family, community, church, ecosystem, planet, or universe—realities that enhance and enrich, not obliterate, the value of the individuals who constitute these larger realities.

Modernity has struggled with the relative values of individual and community. Under modern capitalism we tended to see the

group as an illusion or as the oppressive enemy, always threatening the freedom (or rights) of the individual. (Under modern communism, we tended to do the opposite—to see the individual as
the enemy of the collective, which was the "real" reality, the ultimate value.) Sadly, we Western Christians were so busy struggling
with modernity on other fronts that we were quite overcome by
it in socioeconomic matters. We found ourselves unable to celebrate both the value of the individual and the value of the community. Faced with an either/or rather than a both/and choice, we
voted for the individual. As a result, the biblical story shrank for
us to little more than a simple plan describing how God would
save individual souls from hell. Everything else—the environment,
all human culture, even human history itself—would burn, would
be lost; only individual souls would be salvaged. The ultimate
redemption of all of creation, including our larger group identi-
ties (tribes, nations, languages/cultures), a theme so important in
the Bible, generally evaporated from our thinking about mission.
This reduction led us to boil things down to clever but constricted
statements like mine: "more [individual] Christians and better
[individual] Christians."

Now, in one sense we could say that the "better Christians"
part of a "more Christians/better Christians" mission would
inevitably lead to community, since better Christians will always
pursue love and will thus inevitably create community. But Jesus
presents us with a dream (embodied in the group image "kingdom of God") that is irreducibly communal, familial, and social.
It is not just a dream of more and better individual Christians
standing like isolated statues in a museum. It is a dream of a community vibrant with life, pulsating with forgiveness, loud with celebration, fruitful in mission. The vision of the future it inspires is
not one of individual weightless angels floating on individual
clouds playing individual harps for their own meditative pleasure.
The kingdom vision is a substantial city whose streets bustle with
life, whose buildings echo with praise, a city aglow with the glory
of community.

That is why I now think it is a capitulation to modernity not
to make authentic community an essential strand in the cord of

our mission. Several writers have taken the lead in waking us up to this mission omission, most notably Lesslie Newbigin and the members of the Gospel and Our Culture Network. *The Missional Church* (Eerdmans, 1998), a work whose importance I find hard to exaggerate, demonstrates its message by being a joint work of the GOCN community. The vision they articulate suggests both "mission through community" and "community through mission." The church, they assert, is by nature a missional community—a community that exists by, in, and for mission. But community is not merely utilitarian, a tool for mission. No, the mission itself leads to the creation of an authentic community (aka the kingdom of God), in the Spirit of Jesus Christ.

MY SECOND MISSION OMISSION

*I*f you were reading the previous sentence closely (more closely, I think, than I'd generally like to be read!), you probably noticed that, for me at least, the ultimate community (that is, the community for which the church as a missional community exists) is not just the church itself. In other words, I believe that in the church on the other side we will increasingly see ourselves as existing for something beyond ourselves. We will see the church as a catalyst of a larger reality, which Jesus called the kingdom of God. That's where the phrase "for the good of the world" comes in.

An analogy might help us here. Imagine that we are a modern construction company building a housing development. Our goal: build a great development for the good of our company and the future residents. So we cut down the trees, scrape away the topsoil, fill in the wetlands, channelize the streams, and do whatever else is necessary to build the development. Nearby, we clear-cut and then strip-mine a mountain so that we can get raw materials for our houses and roads. Downstream, silt from our development clogs up a bay. Animals flee or die. Native plants are replaced with ornamental species in black plastic pots. But since none of these problems are visible or bothersome to our residents, we don't notice. It is not that we don't care; it is that we don't notice. We never even think of the larger effects of our development's success. The development's success is our only goal. We finish the development, people move in, and we win awards for an ideal planned community.

This is the church as we have too often practiced it in the modern era. The world exists as a source of raw materials for the church. It's okay to tear people out of their neighborhoods as long as we get them into the church more. It's okay to devalue their "secular" jobs as long as we get them involved in church work more. It's okay to withdraw all our energies from the arts and culture "out there" as long as we have a good choir and nice sanctuary "in here." It's okay because, after all, we're about salvaging individuals from a sinking ship; neighborhoods, economies, cultures, and all but individual human souls will sink, so who cares? In this way of thinking, we could build more Christians, better Christians, and dynamic Christian communities ... at the expense of the world, not for its good.

As we enter the postmodern world, we have to ask ourselves some tough questions: Is the world a mountain to be clear-cut and strip-mined for the benefit of the church? Or is the church a catalyst of blessing for the good of the world? On the other side, you know which answer I believe we must choose.

A SPIRITUAL CRISIS

A few years ago, I was preaching about the struggle between Jesus and the Pharisees. My study created a spiritual crisis for me. In one commentary after another, it seemed, Bible scholars were trying to minimize the degree to which Jesus and the Pharisees were opposed to one another. One commentator seemed apologetic— as if Jesus had overreacted. Why would our scholars seem prone to defend our Lord's worst enemies? Could it be that we are more like them, have more in common with them, feel more kinship with them, than ...? A feeling came over me, like a chill on the back of my neck: Maybe we really are the Pharisees. Maybe, by some absurd twist of history, we Christians have become the very kinds of religious people who would kill Jesus if he showed up today.

For months, I struggled with this conundrum. (Even as I write now, although the feeling isn't as acute, the question remains.) I didn't doubt that I am a Christian, but I began to doubt that any of us Christians are actually Christian. I relate this experience simply to illustrate the importance of our challenge: to reopen the question of what makes a good Christian.

A good Christian as defined in late modernity will differ quite significantly from a good Christian as defined in the postmodern world (just as a good medieval Christian differed from a good modern Christian in many ways). Perhaps there will be no universal description on the other side—but that in itself would mark a change from modernity, where each group assumed *its* "model Christian" was *the* model Christian. We can look back and wonder how anybody's idea of a good Christian could include slave-owning or racism, which were very acceptable in our history (and not so long ago). What will our grandchildren be shocked about when they look at the "good Christians" of our generation? What if, as we move into the postmodern world, we have to go back to the drawing board? What if we need to start from scratch and ask ourselves what it means to be a Christian, as if for the first time, since we are in this new world for the first time? What if we must admit we have become religious in a predictably modern, Western way ... but that we may know next to nothing about what it really means to be followers of Jesus in a new matrix? Are we willing to become as little children and start again?

Will we be willing to admit—in spite of our degrees and books and learning and titles and polemics and radio shows and conferences and opinions and position papers and doctrinal formulations and theological systems and hallowed traditions and strategic plans and statistics that demonstrate beyond any doubt our "effectiveness"—in spite of all these things and more, will we be willing to admit that we are just beginners, neophytes, amateurs, kindergartners, simpletons, and (as Jesus said) "unprofitable servants"? As we move to the other side, this kind of humbling admission will probably be required of us. As we move to the other side, our greatest enemy will not be our ignorance; it will be our unteachability. It won't be what we don't know that threatens us; it will be what we do know. We know too much—so much that we can't learn how much we need to learn. I think you can see what I mean.

3

Practice Systems Thinking

*See the church
program in terms of
interrelated systems rather
than quick fixes.*

*I*magine that you are a zookeeper trying to raise tortoises. (Tortoises are similar to churches in some interesting ways, which you can figure out for yourself.) Tortoises need plenty of calcium to grow, more than most other animals because of their shells. But to metabolize calcium, tortoises need vitamins A and D_3. If they don't have enough of those two vitamins in their diet, it doesn't matter how much calcium they ingest.

One zookeeper is feeding her animals great quantities of calcium and vitamin A, but not enough D_3, so they languish. Then she adds D_3, and within weeks the tortoises are thriving again. She starts spreading the word about the miraculous powers of vitamin D_3, and it turns out that dozens of other zookeepers try it and obtain similar results. Why? Because their tortoises had a similar deficiency. But after a while, the D_3 reaches a maximum level, and now there isn't enough vitamin A. No matter how much D_3 is added, it won't help until A is supplemented. In fact, after some point, the attempts to supplement D_3 may become toxic.

So for a while, D_3 is "the secret." Then it's A. Then A and D_3 are both increased, and more calcium can be metabolized than before—and calcium then becomes the secret. And eventually, limits to growth are reached, so no amount of the secret ingredients will increase the rate of growth or reproduction. In fact, the old secrets may become toxic.

In the old church this kind of systems thinking was rare. Thus, the D3 seminar would hit the circuit, and everyone would flock to it, and it would help some but not others. Then the A movement would hit, leading some people to become "Amatics," and others, "Non-Amatics." And of course, there were the "Calciumatics," who had been beating their drum all along and found that others were finally ready to accept their answer.

In the new church we will be more savvy about program. We will see it as a systems matter. We will realize that churches have certain systems requirements, and what is "the secret" for one church today could be useless for another, if not actually toxic. The program on the other side, then, will not be a single entity, but rather, a new systems approach to program—an approach that anticipates change.

The church's program is the sum of its actions employed to achieve its mission. Now, if in the old church we were uncertain of our mission, we had no standard by which to measure how the program was working. In fact, when we weren't careful, our mission unwittingly became to promote, celebrate, defend, and continue the old program, regardless of its effectiveness. In the new church, guided by our mission, we will have four simple questions by which to evaluate our program:

1. Does this help uncommitted people (including uncommitted people disguised as nominal Christians) become followers of Jesus?
2. Does this help followers of Jesus become *better* followers of Jesus?
3. Does this enhance the development of authentic Christian Community?
4. Does this empower, equip, deploy the church for a missional identity for the good of the world?

COMPLAINTS

There have been many criticisms of the old church program, and as all pastors and elders know, the complaints range from sensible to incoherent to mutually exclusive: It's too boring. It's too enter-tainment-oriented. It's too shallow. It's too deep. It's too intellec-tual. It's too emotional. It's too contemporary. It's too traditional. It's too passive. It's too active. It's too demanding. It's too easy.

In the church on the other side, these complaints will surely continue, because humans are chronic complainers whether they are religious or irreligious. (They just complain about different things.) But there will be a difference. No longer can a parishioner and pastor square off and say, "This is your taste versus mine" (or "your biblical interpretation versus mine," which may be the same thing). In the new church, the mission must become the arbiter in these conflicts. Which approach will help us achieve our mis-sion better? That issue will still be subject to debate, but having a mission to arbitrate such debates is a major step forward—espe-cially when we are open to *both/and* as well as *either/or* answers.

During my lifetime, which has transpired largely in the tran-sition zone between the old and new worlds, we have repeated one very understandable mistake. We have argued over methods, as if old methods are the problem and the sparkling new method will solve the problem. Unfortunately, if a method solves the problem, it will itself become the problem sooner or later when an even newer method will be needed to replace it. This is noth-ing more than the parable of wineskins being replayed again and again.

WHY CHANGE IS HERE TO STAY

So the new church will be relativistic about its program. It will expect change. A certain kind of small group may be the rage for five years, but it will eventually reach its potential and then become incapable of holding the new wine. Then a new kind of group—or midweek service or class or prayer meeting or one-to-one program—will take its place. Worship will evolve from litur-gical to spontaneous and back again. Children's ministry and youth ministry will experience ebbs and flows, innovation and adapta-tion and frustration, in predictable cycles. In the new church, I believe we will stop fighting this fluidity. I think we will *have* to, for at least two reasons.

1. We will realize that each local church must respond to its own internal environment. For example, a new church of 45 people feels silly trying to put on the smooth, "front-focused" program that would be perfectly appropriate for the church of 450 or 4,500. So the small church's internal environment calls for informality. But if the informality is winsome, soon the church will have 85, not 45 . . . then 145, then 245. . . . And by that time, informality will no longer be winsome—it may be chaotic or strained or embarrassing or scary. The church will need to transition to a program that better suits its size. It will have to trade for some new wineskins because of internal changes.

2. We will realize that some external changes will similarly require us to change our programs. The trend today is toward larger and larger churches. However, any number of external changes could make the megachurch less functional: changes in tax laws or energy prices or commuting patterns or real estate prices. Then the trend may reverse. And no doubt it may reverse yet again. The time span for such a cycle may have been 150 years in the old world; it may be fifteen years in the new world—or maybe fifteen months.

In the old church, wineskins were mandates. They couldn't be changed. They were defended as being "the biblical pattern." Denominations enfranchised them, movements dispersed them, seminars marketed them, and companies profited by them. In the new church, we will not only be open to a new program but will loosen up about programs altogether. The leaders of the church will see themselves as the architects of temporary programs, as change agents to help their congregations prepare for changing programs. We won't just trade one old, hallowed program for an alternative hallowed tradition but will accept the notion that no single new program will serve and satisfy us forever.

This difference in approach will entail a cost and a payback. The cost? Change. The payback? Effectiveness. True, not perfect effectiveness, but improved—albeit temporary—effectiveness. These results are inevitable. Clarify your mission—make it easier to adjust your program to achieve your mission—and increased effectiveness is sure to follow. And this is done with God's help, of course, since without grace the whole thing falls flat.

STRATEGY THREE

INTRODUCING SYSTEMS THINKING

*I*n this context, systems thinking has much to offer the church on the other side. Peter Senge introduces systems thinking this way:

> There is something in all of us that loves to put together a puzzle, that loves to see the image of the whole emerge. The beauty of a person, or a flower, or a poem lies in seeing all of it. It is interesting that the words "whole" and "health" come from the same root (the Old English *hal*, as in "hale and hearty"). So it should come as no surprise that the unhealthiness of our world today is in direct proportion to our inability to see it as a whole.
>
> Systems thinking is a discipline for seeing wholes. It is a framework for seeing interrelationships rather than things, for seeing patterns of change rather than static "snapshots." It is a set of general principles—distilled over the course of the twentieth century, spanning fields as diverse as the physical and social sciences, engineering, and management. . . . And systems thinking is a sensibility—for the subtle interconnectedness that gives living systems their unique character. Today, systems thinking is needed more than ever because we are becoming overwhelmed by complexity. . . . Systems thinking is the cornerstone of how learning organizations think about their world.[1]

Systems thinking is an unfolding science. Just reading this chapter might put you far ahead of most people in this regard. Here are some basic observations on systems thinking that seem to have relevance to church life.

1. Systems are interactive in an organism. A malfunction in the nervous system affects the circulatory system, and so on. If there is an infection in the digestive system, the nervous system and the lymphatic system can rush to its aid. Skeletal, nervous, and muscular systems must interact for our bodies to make the most elementary movement. The obvious lesson? Systems should be coordinated. Two systems can be either complementary, destructive, synergistic,

symbiotic, or competitive, and it takes careful design and leadership to keep them coordinated. For example, suppose the pastor of a church preaches that its members should evangelize, but the social and discipleship systems take up all the members' free time so they have precious little personal contact with nonbelievers. This means that the evangelistic, missional and fellowship discipleship systems are competitive, not synergistic.

2. Systems experience limits to growth. A mouse can grow to only a certain size. Even an elephant can grow only so large. However, both mice and elephants can multiply, so the total biomass of each species has nearly unlimited growth potential. Churches are a lot like mice and elephants. Some are small; others are big. The potential for growth is unlimited. But as with mice and elephants, sometimes no amount of coaxing can cause a church to grow beyond a certain size. To get more growth you must either exchange one type for another or have the church multiply, reproducing more of its own kind. Consider the common scenario of a church whose attendance has been level for several years. Then, because of either an unwanted church split or an intentional church-planting endeavor, the number of attenders is cut in half. Frequently such a church will grow fairly quickly and return to its original size—but no larger. Because the limits to growth have not been removed, the church cannot grow beyond its previous limit.

Carl George explores the critical interactions between size and growth in many of his books.[2] (Among other things he describes certain barriers of attendance at the levels of 200, 400, 800, and so on.)

3. Vigorous systems reproduce in various ways. Some reproduction comes by division, as in cell mitosis or in the budding of plants. Other organisms have complex reproductive strategies, involving gene pools, diversity with unity, courtship, stimulation, excitement, attraction—even love. In these cases, systems tend to reproduce after their kind; the new generation resembles the old.

But sometimes a system can reproduce in reaction against the parent system. For example, some churches (and denominations) display an amazing, energetic, enthusiastic, resilient, confident, indefatigable, and smothering rigidity. Creativity and innovation are shunned like apostasy and adultery. The elders of the tribe resemble the dominant males of a pride of lions on the Serengeti. In spite of their august manes and stately bearing, these "kings" seem to be threatened by all up-and-comers; so with survival-of-the-fittest determination, the older drive the younger away. Such innovation-averse organizations guarantee that the brightest and best of the next generation will leave and create new "prides" in new territories (or in their own back yard). Having been thus rebuffed, the leaders of these new prides often want to be as different as possible from their parent organizations. Thus the least creative parent churches (or denominations) unintentionally become the parents of the most creative new churches (or denominations), which display reproduction against their kind. One way or another, then—whether after their kind or in reaction to their kind—vigorous systems reproduce.

4. Systems must eliminate waste and fight disease. A system will discontinue if it loses the ability to neutralize or discharge baggage, toxins, stress, germs, and waste products. Many churches languish or die because they have no way to rid themselves of destructive elements that have invaded or developed in the body.

5. Systems require infusions of energy. Since entropy—the loss of heat or energy—is a fact of life, each system needs some form of nourishment. The form of nourishment depends on the system; it could be learning, encouragement, correction, guidance, attention, money, voluntarism, recognition, fun, or celebration. Many churches haven't learned what energizes them, so they function with chronic fatigue.

6. Systems are often under external attack. Sometimes what doesn't destroy the system actually makes it stronger—as when a body produces antibodies to ward off a disease, or when a country unifies under the threat of a military invasion. Sometimes the energy of the attacker can be turned back on him. Sometimes the system's reaction to attack can be more destructive than the attack itself, as is often seen when churches or organizations, reacting to criticism, react in ways that become self-destructive over time.

7. Systems often perform recycling and multiple functions. A tree produces oxygen, inhibits erosion, cools the forest floor,

provides a home for birds and animals, and after it dies, enriches the soil, which nourishes the next generation of trees. Sunday schools and small-group ministries similarly fulfill multiple functions in a church: training children and adults, providing leadership experience, creating many roles for the use of spiritual gifts, promoting social interaction, encouraging mutual care, providing contexts for singles to find mates, and creating affinity subgroups to promote diversity in the congregation at large.

8. Systems often benefit from diversity. A field planted with corn (a monoculture) has certain advantages and benefits, but a rain forest (containing thousands of diverse species) can be much more productive and sustainable. The body analogy in Scripture (Romans 12; 1 Corinthians 12) explores one dimension of this diversity. Debates about the "homogenous unit principle" and the stubborn tenacity of voluntary racial segregation among churches suggest other dimensions. Not all diversity is helpful, of course. A diversity of sheep and wolves or ticks and dogs benefits some parties at the expense of others.

9. Systems tend either toward achieving a sustainable balance or toward disorder. We call that balance "health" and the ultimate disorder "death." Interestingly, systems sometimes throw themselves out of balance on purpose, as in the case of vomiting or fever or depression. This temporary imbalance becomes necessary to ensure long-term balance and survival in the presence of some real or perceived threat.

10. Systems often react to both external and internal changes. Systems can overreact and underreact. They can react too quickly or too slowly. A system's mode of reaction affects its success. The "frog in the kettle" analogy (the idea that a frog could unknowingly be scalded to death by your gradually heating up the water he sits in) or the processes of evolution and extinction are clear examples of this principle, which has a thousand applications to church life.

11. Leaders require some degree of differentiation from the system itself. Like a head on a living animal, leaders need connection (a neck) that allows for some distance. Much pastoral burnout results from a failure to self-differentiate effectively. (A

valuable book in this regard is rabbi Edwin Friedman's *Generation to Generation: Family Systems in Church and Synagogue*, New York: Guilford Press, 1985).

12. Systems can become sick. We speak of dysfunctional and codependent family systems. Sick systems can have remarkable staying power—sometimes appearing even stronger than healthy ones. Fanatical religious groups and cults can be viewed as sick but strong systems.

13. Fractals are often characteristic of large systems. In some crystalline rock formations, each fragment (or fractal) that is broken off from the parent rock will have the same shape as the parent. The smaller units seem to organize themselves into larger units of the same shape—or conversely put, the organizing principle of the larger unit shows itself in the smaller units. Some local churches can be seen as fractals of their denomination, with the same conflicts and dynamics as the larger structure to which they belong.

14. Systems must be seen as part of the larger wholes in which they function. To understand an organism's digestive system properly, we must consider not only its related circulatory and nervous systems, but also its relation to the body as a whole. Is the body sick or healthy, thin or obese, happy or depressed, at peace or distressed? And really, one must go further: The body that it serves is part of larger family systems, economic systems, and ecological systems that have various interactions with the digestive system under consideration. Is the family Mexican or Scottish, prone to cook spicy foods or bland? Is the surrounding economy poor or rich, at peace or at war, involved in international trade or economically insular? Does this person live in a polluted environment, and are the soils of the surrounding countryside fertile or depleted of nutrients? All these affect the stomach and intestines we may be studying. Similarly, to understand a church properly, we need to think of the many wholes the church participates in—historical, cultural, economic, political, and educational.

Insights like these arising from systems thinking will go a long way toward helping the church on the other side evaluate and improve its program. They will, if we explore and use them, help our churches become learning organizations whose programs can adapt and thus remain supportive of the ultimate mission for which our churches exist: more Christians, better Christians, in authentic community, for the good of the world.

MORE IN COMMON THAN WE THINK

I grew up in a small Christian nondenomination (a nondenominational denomination) that defined itself by its nonprogram. Its liturgy was nonliturgical. Its clergy was nonclerical. Its book of order was nonwritten. As an adult, I was for several years part of a large Episcopal church, whose program was much more overt. (For a time I planned on becoming an Episcopal priest.) In between, as an adolescent, I was part of the Jesus Movement in the early seventies. So over the years I have been around the Christian block a good bit. I have seen many different systems at work in many different kinds of churches.

I am struck far more by the similarities than the differences. In spite of our different doctrines, history, polity, liturgy, architecture, and constituencies, we experience common sociologies. We have common systems. For example, whether a church is independent, informally associated, presbyterian, or episcopal in its structure, it has leadership protocols, checks and balances of various forms, and ways and codes to gain and lose power—all part of its leadership system.

Whether a church is charismatic or noncharismatic, there are certain signs and wonders that it naturally has in view and that its programs are designed to promote. They also nourish its system— whether it's an aesthetic moment in a Bach prelude that takes your breath away, or an emotional rush of warmth as a new believer shares her testimony, or a miraculous answer to prayer regarding a financial need, or a homeless man who is given lodging for another winter night, or a person speaking in tongues, or an experience of intimacy, trust, and vulnerability in a group of tough working men.

We have catechism systems for children, outreach and assimilation systems for growth, discipline systems for misbehavior or

STRATEGY THREE

misbelief, stewardship systems for finances, reward systems for volunteers, and so on. Some of our systems are written down and clearly defined, as in the Episcopal church; many of them are not, as in the church of my youth. And many of our best systems we probably don't even recognize as such, while many of our paper programs aren't worth the paper they're written on.

Learning about one another's programs will help us, as we uncover similarities and differences beneath the surface, to see the deeper systems issues at work in all churches. When we see our church programs in those larger systems terms, we can make huge strides toward greater effectiveness. That's one of many ways in which closer relationships across denominational and cultural lines will help us help one another make it to the other side. We might not make it alone.

Trade Up Your Traditions
for Tradition

*Distinguish between church
traditions and the Christian
Tradition, and move emphasis
from the former to the latter.*

One of the worst days of my life occurred in my early twenties. The girl I loved and was engaged to marry told me she was still in love with her old boyfriend. This occurred early on the morning after our engagement party—at which we had been given at least three toasters, an electric frying pan, bath towels, and other items that tend to solemnize and solidify a relationship.

Stunned, I rushed out of her mother's house, where we were staying, and walked the streets of that little town for hours, cussing and praying, angry and broken-hearted. It was a Sunday morning, and I was barefoot, wearing jeans and the usual holey (not holy) T-shirt, my teeth unbrushed, my longish hair combed only by my fingers. In spite of my attire, my desperate emotional state made me want to go sit in a church.

I had passed a church a few blocks back, but—having also left without my watch—I had no idea what time it was. The streets were strangely vacant. I saw one man trimming hedges a few blocks down the road. I walked up to him and asked, "Excuse me, do you know what time it is?" "I think about nine-fifteen," he answered. "Let me go inside and check."

"That's not necessa—" I began, but he had already bounded up the steps.

"I was wrong," he said, returning. "It's almost ten."

"Thanks," I replied, and I started padding away in my bare feet. Did I mention that it was October and I was shivering?

"Just a minute," he called out to me. "Do you need to talk?" He had no idea. I would have started crying, but I was shivering too hard.

I asked him, "Are you a Christian?"

"Yes."

He invited me inside, and this stranger gave me a cup of hot coffee (God bless that man!). He and his wife and ten-year-old son sat there at the kitchen table and listened to my sad story. Then they prayed for me—all three of them, even the ten-year-old. By that time I had stopped shivering enough to cry.

They were Roman Catholics. Charismatics. I was a Plymouth Brethren boy, belonging to a group not famous for its acceptance of fellow Protestants, much less papists—and certainly not *charismatics*. But around that kitchen table, I knew we were one. Need brought us together—my need. Funny thing: It was a bad day, but a good memory.

(And the girl I loved ended up working through her feelings, and we got married, and in the last twenty-some years we have worn out all three toasters, the electric frying pan, and most of the bath towels we were given at our engagement party, with the help of our four kids, of course—all sure signs of a lasting relationship.)

I think something similar is happening between here and the other side. In my lifetime I have seen signs of a remarkable trend toward breaking down denominational barriers among Christians. The gene pool is being enriched, the gardens are being cross-pollinated, and everyone stands to benefit much.

Perhaps this is happening because we have encountered almost more change than we can handle. Isn't there a point at which we reach future shock, change paralysis, rootlessness? One more change, and we'll go over the edge. Isn't there a legitimate longing for stability, memories, heritage—for, dare we say it, a new tradition?

But isn't "new tradition" an oxymoron? Will there even be tradition on the other side? Isn't tradition exactly what has caused us so many problems in the old church? To answer these questions, it is probably worth our making a fine distinction, between traditions (plural) and tradition (singular).

The plural form of the noun deals with specific acts, rites, rituals, behaviors, and quirks that have meaning to a particular group. In her book *Worship Evangelism* (which is helping a lot of people move toward the other side), Sally Morgenthaler says this of traditions (plural):

> Traditions are a dangerous but persistent fact of life. Just when we think we have rid ourselves of them, we have already formed new ones. The problem is, which ones do we discard, which ones are "keepers," and what do we do with the "keepers" to preserve their significance?[1]

In the church on the other side we will all have to do a lot of this kind of sorting and handling of traditions, with an *s*. But even more important than what we do with Christian traditions (plural) is what we will do with "the Christian tradition" (singular)—which has to do with the doctrines, history, heroes, disciplines, moral codes, and art accumulated until our transition to the other side.

DOMINOES AND MUTUAL FUNDS

*P*aradoxically, in the midst of all the chaotic change of transitioning to the new world, I believe we are well placed to rediscover the stabilizing value, the awesome richness, of "the Christian tradition." Sadly, in the waning years of the old world, especially among Protestants, we were rich in traditions and poor in the tradition. We were a group of competitive sects, lined up like so many dominoes on their short, wobbly ends—each of us proud of our distinct configuration of white dots, each conscious of our differentness from all the other dominoes, each almost unaware of how much we had in common, each vulnerable to toppling. Perhaps that's what is happening in the transition zone—we are toppling in our separateness. And just maybe, as we find ourselves toppled together on the table, we can be reconfigured, reconnected, and interlocked like bricks, to offer something more substantial as our inheritance to the new church.

Or, to change the metaphor, in the old world we were like a group of misers, each with his little sock full of inheritance money hidden away in a drawer somewhere. Our sectarian traditions—our distinctive doctrines, our denominational histories, our proprietary heroes, our characteristic disciplines, our idiosyncratic moral codes, our private art museums—were being used up, and we saw ourselves going broke. In the transition zone, it seems, we are coming together out of desperation with our pathetic little socks in hand, emptying them out into one pile. And we are discovering that our meager stashes can combine to form a huge mutual fund, miraculously greater than the sum of its parts. We are finding that by trying to save our little sliver of tradition for ourselves, we were losing it, but that by losing it—by giving it up into one bigger Christian tradition—we are gaining so much more.

What do we gain when we trade in our little heritage and rediscover "the Christian tradition" on the other side?

1. TRADING UP DOCTRINE

*W*e trade our doctrinal statements—some wispy, some flabby—for a well-toned body of common sense: time-tested doctrine, lean and muscular, stripped of its fat and scrubbed clean of its cosmetics. In other words, in the new church we will have a common bank account of essential Christian beliefs.

In the old world we were so preoccupied with our distinctive domino dots that we didn't realize we had the same shape and the same color and were even playing the same game. But as the differences between committed Christians and the rest of society grow more and more obvious—as we compare ourselves to darts and playing cards and pool cues, for example—we gradually realize how much we dominoes have in common.

True, the church on the other side will have its share of doctrinal squabbles to keep it from growing bored. After all, we humans seldom indulge in too much uninterrupted harmony for very long! But with so many peripheral issues changing at the

STRATEGY FOUR

fringes, we will need to affirm the core beliefs that hold us together as never before.

Whoever articulates these core beliefs in contemporary language, whoever helps us see the basic shape of what we're becoming, whoever does so in a compelling and attractive and accurate way—that person will be doing a great service to the new church.

2. TRADING UP HISTORY

*W*e will trade in our private histories for one grand, shared history. Over the horizon of the new world, we will cherish not the memories of our little splintered clans, but the story of a whole tribe. Clinging to our little histories—whether Methodist, Brethren, Mennonite, Reformed Presbyterian, or Baptist—is like guppies trying to feel big in little bowls. In the new church we will empty out all our little stale bowls and discover a broad, windy ocean of memories to swim in. We will see that although the names and datelines were different, the same dynamics were at work in all our little histories, the same psychologies, the same sociologies, the same dark pathologies and blushing embarrassments. And oddly enough, those embarrassments will probably do us more good than the inspirations, since the more humble we feel, the better prepared we are to receive abounding grace.

On the other side, then, we will see the broader scope of our shared history as Christians. We won't pretend, as many Protestant churches have done, that true Christian history began at the first Christmas, then went into a coma in the second or third century, and awoke from its sleep with the dawn of our glorious denomination (whether that was 1518, 1639, 1833, or 1908). We won't fall into thinking that God can't keep track of east and west at the same time, or that he can't see his people without first looking through the filters of our hierarchies. In other words, in the new church, our Roman, Orthodox, and Protestant historical bank accounts will seem more like one combined mutual fund.

True, we won't learn all from our history that we should or could, but the advantage of combining our historical assets will humble us, challenge us, and help us earn at least a little better return on investment than we used to in the old world.

3. TRADING UP HEROES

 We will trade our short list of sectarian heroes for a longer, stronger, better list of Christian heroes. As a "baby boomer" I have been at many a party where we boomers reminisce about the early days of television and its heroes. If young people are present, they don't even know whom we're talking about (unless our heroes have been resurrected in reruns); in the same way, these young-sters tell us aging kids about heroes we have never even heard of. And we argue whose heroes are better. So it's Mighty Mouse (complete with an opera soundtrack) versus the Teenage Mutant Ninja Turtles (cowabunga!), the Lone Ranger (da-da-da, da-da-da, da-da-da, da-DA) against the Power Rangers (it's morphin' time!), Gilligan (surviving cheerfully, shipwrecked on his island) versus Jean-Luc Picard (boldly going where no one has gone before). Whether we find them in television, sports, politics, or religion, we all have our heroes, and we like to argue about whose heroes are the best.

In the old world, our spiritual heroes were similarly propri-etary. The Methodists would say, "John Wesley is ours; you can't have him!" The Presbyterians would respond, "That Arminian? We wouldn't want him! John Calvin is our man!" "Calvin?" the Lutherans would reply, "He was just Robin to our Batman, Mar-tin Luther! There's a real hero for you!" Meanwhile, the Roman Catholics would rise from their couch and join the fray: "And what about St. Francis? Or Mother Teresa?" "Well," the Baptists respond, "we do have Billy Graham." The Mennonites, never too quick to interrupt, now offer, "Then there is Menno Simons. . . ." (Some devotees of televangelism start whispering, "Who? Menno? What kind of name is that?" They have been strangely silent through all this and were about to mention their favorite toupeed evangelist, but then thought the better of it.)

In the new church we will realize that, like Paul and Apollos in the early church, all these heroes are our heroes. And transition zone leaders like Billy Graham and Bill Hybels and Mother Teresa are teaching us that it's not only yesterday's heroes who form our common heritage, but today's heroes also. Together they will be invaluable assets in our common Christian tradition on the other side.

4. TRADING UP SPIRITUALITY

Similarly, we will trade up in the matter of spirituality, contributing our snacks of loaves and fishes—our discrete spiritualities and distinctive spiritual disciplines—and gaining a veritable five-course spiritual feast in return.

For example, on the other side, one local church may, in one month's time and through various venues during the week, offer for its congregation's spiritual enrichment the following: a Quaker-style meditation service, a Brethren-style communion service, a healing service derived from charismatic Episcopalians, weekend seeker services à la Willow Creek, a silent retreat with fasting at a Benedictine monastery, a lecture series comparing Calvin's *Institutes* and Aquinas's *Summa*, and more. Meanwhile, the church will encourage private journaling (inspired by Roman Catholic mystics), shared experiments with living in community (inspired by the Jesus People), short-term missionary service in an inner-city neighborhood (the influence of the Salvation Army or of the social gospel?), a public demonstration for racial reconciliation (in the tradition of Martin Luther King, Jr.), and a field trip to an art gallery to enjoy an exhibit of Byzantine iconography. The following month, there may be an evangelism class (showing the influence of Campus Crusade), an inductive Bible study class (InterVarsity Christian Fellowship), a class in personal Bible study and memorization (the Navigators), and a class in Christian literature (studying Catholic writers Flannery O'Connor, Walker Percy, Thomas Merton, and Henri Nouwen).

Does all this suggest schizophrenia? Multiple personality disorder? Relativism? An identity crisis? No, this will be the expression of a normal, healthy sense of the Christian spiritual tradition on the other side. We have many good writers to thank for cross-pollinating and bringing diverse streams of Christian spirituality to a wider audience. Regent College founder James Houston[2] and Richard Foster (through his Renovare program and his many books)[3] are two of the best.

We should be deeply grateful for them and those other "scribes of the kingdom" who "bring forth treasures new and old" (Matthew 13:52). Many of us are waiting for a new high tide to come in. From a low tide of dead orthodoxy and dreary routine, we have seen the tide change to a shallow spirituality of foam and zest—exciting, but too often trite, unstable, formulaic, fad-driven, banal. We look forward to a deeper, stronger, high-tide spirituality—no less exciting, but enriched by the very best of our profound and largely ignored common heritage (in music, liturgy, spiritual disciplines, and devotional literature). Let the high tide come in!

5. TRADING UP MORAL AGENDAS

On the other side, we will exchange both our "Trivial Pursuit" moral agenda and our "new morality" nonagenda for a rediscovery of basic, time-tested Christian morality.

We who have lived through the last three decades of the transition zone should have learned at least three things:

a. Societies and individuals alike need healthy families. Two-parent, heterosexual families, whenever possible, are a pretty good idea after all.

b. Such families depend on solvent marriages, and, we have discovered, staying the course "till death do us part" is tough under the best of circumstances. Therefore, we are finding that tolerating infidelity and sexual indiscretions is like running a marathon with wine cooler in our water bottle or bathroom slippers on our feet—they possess a certain adolescent appeal perhaps, but they are patently stupid in the long run if we intend to finish the race.

c. If we want to have a good life, we sooner or later have to surrender to the remarkable concept of being—surprise of surprises—a good person.

In contrast, many of us grew up in the old-world church where the moral sun rose and set on what now seems trivial: Should women wear headcoverings over their hair? Can they have short hair, and men long? Can guitars be used in worship? *Drums?* Can one watch television on Sunday? Eat red meat on Friday? Can a man worship without a tie? Can a woman speak in a public service, and if so, when, where, and how? (Meanwhile, Mr. Jones hasn't spoken to Mr. Nelson since their wives had that spat seventeen years ago. And meanwhile, when blacks showed up at our all-white church, they were referred to a "colored" church in our denomination downtown. And meanwhile . . .)

In the new church, we won't have the luxury of these kinds of moral mousehunts. I believe we will be a little more basic: Can we please stay out of bed with people we aren't married to? Can the Christians of the world agree to stop killing each other over petty political issues? Could our faith by chance overcome our racism? Might we actually make friends with a needy neighbor of another cultural or demographic background, Good Samaritan-style? Husbands, will you stop beating (or browbeating) your wives—now? And parents . . . And about forgiveness . . .

True, between here and the other side we have a few huge moral issues to face, including abortion and homosexuality. But even these difficult areas (difficult to resolve in practice, even if we think they're clear in theory) may fall into place. Seeing our moral struggles, two very unlikely forces have graciously stepped in to help us deal with them: the media and lawyers.

Unlikely Prophets

The media have helped us by uncovering our sexual and financial scandals, by shining their flashlights under our covers, leafing through our IRS returns, publicizing our behind-closed-door deals, and broadcasting our hypocrisies. Some of us used to think we could indulge in private immoralities (alcohol or drug abuse, sexual misconduct, financial malfeasance) as long as we took a strong stand on public issues (poverty, racism, war). Some of us thought the reverse—that a little racism or sexism was no big deal as long as we stayed in the right bed. Too many of us thought we could do just about anything as long as we said the right things and didn't get exposed.

But the media have virtually fulfilled Jesus' prophecy about things said and done in secret being broadcast from the housetops (see Matthew 10:26–27). They have taught us what we had ignored in our great Christian moral tradition: that we need to integrate both public morality and private morality to have something called "integrity."

The lawyers then stopped by to help us in a second way. As lawsuits were filed dealing with clergy pedophilia and clergy sexual harassment (whether hetero- or homosexual in orientation), churches had no choice but to get serious about at least their leaders returning to Ten Commandments–style morality, for legal and public-relations reasons if not for moral conviction. And if the leaders must become more traditionally moral, the people in their congregations probably will, too. Isn't it interesting how history has a way of being self-correcting? And think of it: the media and lawyers, like a rewriting of the Balaam story!

So in the new church, in spite of the unsolved dilemmas of abortion, homosexuality, and the like, we may just find ourselves united as never before in trying to help our people toward moral living, in public and in private. We will realize what wonderful assets we had in the Christian tradition all along: the Ten Commandments, the Sermon on the Mount, the Love Chapter (1 Corinthians 13). And maybe, just maybe, we'll accept this modest proposal: that for, say, the next twenty-five years we will dedicate 95 percent of our moral effort toward living these basic, unarguable elements of our moral tradition. Then we can reevaluate and see whether the other issues—the trivial questions and the big dilemmas alike—have taken care of themselves. Even if they haven't, with twenty-five years of moral exercise we will be better equipped to address them with . . . integrity.

6. TRADING UP ART

*L*ast but not least, in the new church we will reappraise the value of the artistic dimension of our Christian tradition.

Granted, of late we might not have much to be proud of. Late old-world evangelical Protestantism, for example, if it were memorialized in an art museum, would too often be forgettable and not worth free admission. Imagine the artifacts: mustard seeds in cubes of clear plastic (sculpture), windowless metal buildings with artificial-brick façades (architecture), wall-mounted, pressed-muck plaques with Scripture verses on them (painting), Christian romance novels or demon-oriented horror novels (fiction), how-to-help-yourself books (nonfiction), and end-of-the-world evangelistic movies (film).

But step back a little and think of the incredible resource we have, from the fugues of Bach to the Chronicles of Narnia, from medieval drama to a contemporary sketch from Handel's *Messiah*, from a quaint little chapel in the hills of Pennsylvania to a grand European cathedral, from Gregorian chants to Bruce Cockburn and black gospel music, from serene liturgical dance to a serendipitous Pentecostal shuffle. What diversity! What energy! What depth! What glory! And in the new church, it will all be ours, our common resource, our shared heritage—our Christian tradition.

True, in our first twenty centuries as Christians, we produced some schlock, some truly pathetic moments. But, inspired by the miracle of the Incarnation, we also produced beauty. As Robert Webber has said:

> What [the Incarnation] means for the arts is that the divine chooses to become present through creation, through wood, stone, mortar, color, sound, shape, form, movement, and action. Christians are not Gnostics. We do not reject the body, the material, the tangible. To do so would be to reject the Incarnation.[4]

Perhaps the paucity of our art in recent decades is a sign that we had lost touch with the great Christian Tradition and had run aground in the shallow tributaries of our narrow little traditions. In the new church we must get ourselves unstuck and rediscover the broad horizons and deep resources of our tradition, in all the matters we have looked at: our doctrinal and intellectual resources, our historical perspectives, our inspiring heroes, our rich and diverse spirituality, our time-tested moral code and vision, and yes, our art. Reconnected with these resources, rerooted in our Tradition, change in our traditions will be a lot easier to bear.[5]

Resurrect Theology as Art and Science

Stop thinking of theology as a matter of technical training, in which answers are already known, and rejuvenate theology through a quest for truth and beauty.

To say that the church on the other side needs a new theology is not to suggest heresy. It is simply to distinguish between the message (God's truth, revelation, action, and expression) and theology (our task, our work, our language, our search to understand and articulate God's message). In the old church we too often forgot that the two are different. We were aware how other people had confused the two, but seldom considered how we might have done so. In the new church we will try harder to remember that God is God and we are mere creatures, and that our attempts to understand and articulate his message and truth are always approximations.

DOING THEOLOGY

When we "do theology," we are clay pots pondering the potter, kids pondering their father, ants discussing the elephant. At some level of profundity and accuracy, we are bound to be inadequate or incomplete all the time, in almost anything we say or think, considering our human limitations, including language, and God's infinite greatness. Thus the noblest and loftiest thing we can do— which is to consider our Creator—always should humble us even as it ennobles us. As a father of four, I think of times when I have overheard my kids talking about me: what I meant by something I said, how I felt about things, what I really wanted them to do. Sometimes what they said was more or less true; other times, completely wrong or twisted or even cute. That's what we are like doing theology.

In the new church we can do a little better job if we remember that our words are not the things they represent. We will try to remember that; as wonderful, useful, and powerful as they are, words are merely sounds and symbols that stimulate some kind of remarkably predictable and similar neurological activity in the brains of our peers, our words are not the Word.

These kinds of distinctions can liberate us both from and in our systematic theologies. They can liberate us from all systematic theologies in the absolute sense. That is, we can step back and realize that Systematic Theology X, as admirably as it addresses problems 1 to 7, doesn't help us much on problems 8 to 11; we are free to critique it or even respectfully differ with it because, after all, Systematic Theology X embraces human words, not God's Word. Yet these distinctions also dignify systematic theology by challenging us to improve our attempts to understand and articulate the Word in our words. In so doing, moreover, the new church may help put systematic theologians and artists and scientists back into fellowship, since each is trying to understand and articulate God's truth and message and self-expression in some way.

NEVER FINISHED?

That association is key to this strategy. We don't expect artists and scientists to "finish." We don't expect anyone at long last to paint "the right painting" or to finally complete scientific inquiry with the last discovery. Yet somehow we have thought that theologians either had or were about to finish theology—cross the final *t* and correct the final misconception—as if God were a more limited realm than science and art! In the new church, if we readjust our expectations and allow theology, like science and art, to continue in an unending exploration and eternal search for the truth, good-

STRATEGY FIVE

ness, and beauty of God and his relation to our universe and all it contains—then theology will be wonderfully resurrected for us. This new approach to theology won't be just another new theology, nor even a new paradigm of theology; rather, it will be a new paradigm for doing theology.

This new approach is necessary because, I believe, we live in a time when the old systematic theologies are fading. They are not surviving the transition time well. Calvinism (or neo-Calvinism) is probably the strongest and most virile of all the systems, but even that is showing signs of defensiveness in many quarters that expose its decline. Actually, I think the new theology has been, in some seminal form, alive and well among us already for quite some time. In the middle of the twentieth century C. S. Lewis expressed early articulations of it in essays and, even better, in fiction. By the end of the century, one feels the new theology moving in Roman Catholics such as Brennan Manning, Romano Guardini, Henri Nouwen, and Pope John Paul II, and in Protestants such as Richard Foster, Dallas Willard, Leonard Sweet, Lesslie Newbigin, and the later Billy Graham.

KILLING THEOLOGY BY ACCIDENT

If one believes that the systematic theology par excellence has already been achieved and perfectly articulated for all time (whether in Calvinism or Dispensationalism or Liberation Theology or whatever), then in a sense that person kills theology as a scholarly pursuit and turns seminaries into technical schools. Only where there is a need for creativity and problem solving do we find life. If all problems have theoretically been solved, and if everything worth saying has been said as well as it can be, then theology is dead, whether God lives or not! Of course, no one in the old theology would say it so crassly. Many have noted the listlessness and boredom of seminary education in recent years and have bemoaned its drift toward arid theory or touchy-feely psychology or organizational management devoted to the bottom line. Perhaps these were signs that theology itself didn't have much to keep itself busy, on the assumption that it had pretty well mapped out the Word in its own terms.

In the church on the other side , then, for better or worse, I think theology must come back to life—and not just as a technical matter, but as a creative pursuit and passionate inquiry, like the best art and the best science. Psychology, sociology, the new physics, history, comparative religion, and spirituality—not to mention postmodernism in general—all are calling for some creative Christian theologians to unfold some new paradigms for us to use in our explorations. The old systems feel tired, used up, old hat, and worn, but the thirst for God is as strong as ever. New theological wineskins? I think so; I hope so. What a change occurs in the atmosphere of a seminary when we see the theologian as the creative thinker, the pursuer of truth, the wholehearted seeker and explorer and learner, rather than the memorizer, repeater, and defender of old formulations. What a challenge we encounter when we open ourselves to discover how Jesus Christ wants to theologically incarnate himself for the postmodern world, just as he did for the post-Enlightenment world of the old church.

GETTING HONEST

*I*t has been fashionable among the innovative pastors I know to say, "We're not changing the message; we're only changing the medium." This claim is probably less than honest in this transition zone, and it will be downright wrong on the other side, for at least two reasons.

First, in the new church we must realize how medium and message are intertwined. When we change the medium, the message that's received is changed, however subtly, as well. We might as well get beyond our naïveté or denial about this.

Second, in the new church we will be aware that our message is not perfect. God's message is perfect; but all of our versions of it are always to some degree out of sync with his version. To the degree that we are trying to get our message straight, we have to admit that there is some need for changing it. This is a risky, dangerous enterprise, with much at stake. For this reason, theology in the new church is more important, not less important, than in the old church, which felt that it already had the message straight and simply needed to proclaim and defend it.

But, you ask, won't this theological activity simply result in more conflict? Won't it simply plunge us into more schism?

Perhaps. Even probably. But maybe not. If, in the new paradigm of theology, we keep trusting that the Word beneath our words is there, if we lean on God and not on our own understanding (even our own understanding of God), if we can doubt ourselves and our cogitation while we trust in the living God who is with us, if our hearts are right—then maybe we can have creativity and truth-seeking without jailing so many Galileos, burning so many John Huses, damning so many Martin Luthers and Martin Luther Kings, and thus pruning off the green growth at the ends of our branches.

We have one factor in our favor in the new world: Nobody has that much power anymore. And I think it is power that makes us into Pharisees who see Jesus as a threat. We don't control governments; our denominations aren't monolithic; we have to tolerate diversity in nonessentials so as to enjoy unity in the essentials. So maybe the new theology, the "mere Christianity," the "catholic evangelicalism" or the "evangelical catholicism" that many have spoken of—maybe it will feel like Jesus, young and vigorous, bursting onto the scene with a parable on its lips, a whip in its hands, a sparkle in its eyes, and joy in its voice.

Such a new theology might just awaken some slumbering Christians. What is equally exciting, it might attract some of our disinterested and unbelieving friends and neighbors, too. (But that gets us into the next strategy, which deals with apologetics.)

FRIGHTENING—BUT NECESSARY

*W*riting this chapter frightens me, as does writing the chapters on postmodernism (Strategy 12). I was studying literature in graduate school just as postmodernism was making its debut. Beginning in literary criticism, it spread out to affect almost every other discipline. The same forces that spawned postmodernism in the academy were already at work on the street, and I know that the full impact of postmodernism is still far beyond my comprehension. I have read hundreds of pages of Christian attempts to deal with postmodernism, and I put down each book saying to myself, "Okay, good start, some good points, but we're just scratching the surface."

Postmodernism is the intellectual boundary between the old world and the other side. Why is it so important? Because when your view of truth is changed, when your confidence in the human ability to know truth in any objective way is revolutionized, then everything changes. That includes theology—and not only the content of your theology, nor only its categories. More far-reaching, the mind of the person doing and learning theology is also changed. We have the same basic data—but different software and different hardware. And that changes everything.

I read an interview with a popular Christian apologist a few years back. He was asked what he thought of postmodernism, and he answered something like this: "It must be opposed at all costs." There came the followup question: Why? "Because it destroys our apologetic."

I thought, Thank God this guy is over sixty—he can afford to think that postmodernism can be opposed. But for me and those younger than I, opposing postmodernism is as futile as opposing the English language. It's here. It's reality. It's the future. It's not only a fact on the event horizon; it's the way my generation processes every other fact on the event horizon. What are we going to do about it, with it, in it?

So one of the biggest questions on my screen these days is, How does the Spirit of Jesus Christ incarnate in a postmodern world? This question very likely terrifies or infuriates some Christians because they see the traumatic implications of what I am saying (and will say more about in Strategy 12). And maybe they are right: Maybe there is no way ahead. Maybe the faithful thing to do these days is to become intellectually Amish and create communities that live in the past.

But in spite of my fear, I have this faith—that if we push forward through this transition time, some of us may find a good land for Christian faith on the other side. It will require courage, creativity, honesty, humility. It will require that Christian theologians become more like the best artists and scientists—passionately devoted to truth, and less like politicians—concerned about institutions and alliances and reelection (tenure) and book sales. I am an amateur pastor and a hack theologian, but I care about truth, and I try to think from time to time. If these lines of thought seem important to me, how much more should they inspire those with the primary calling to theology. May God give them the courage to step out of the boat and walk on water, to lead the way in our journey to the other side.

Design a New Apologetic

*Find fresh ways to
communicate the gospel
to the postmodern mind.*

A few years ago I was invited by a friend to speak to
a group of visiting scholars from the People's
Republic of China. I was asked to speak on the existence
of God. The lecture took place at the University of
Maryland, where I used to teach English before I
became a minister full time. These scholars had been
through the cultural revolution, and then had experienced the Chinese version of *Glasnost*, and then had felt
their world tighten again after the Tienanmen Square
incident. I imagine it must have taken some courage to
attend a lecture on this topic. But the attendance was
good—about forty, as I remember.

Rather than argue for the existence of God, I felt I
should take a different approach. I titled my lecture,
"How to Think About the Existence of God." Instead of
arguing for the existence of God, I presented a series of
questions one would naturally need to consider in the
search for God, with a kind of tree diagram to illustrate
possible answers to each question. I tried to be somewhat objective and give each option a fair hearing, and
then I explained which answers I had chosen in my own
life, working my way down the tree diagram to the
Christian faith. I also shared a personal story of how my
faith had helped me deal with a difficult personal experience, when my son was diagnosed with leukemia. I
told them I hoped these thoughts had been helpful, and
then opened the floor for questions.

A distinguished gentleman stood, with Asian respect, to ask his question: "Sir, I do not have a question, but I wish to thank you on behalf of all of us. You have helped us a great deal. Instead of telling us what to believe, you have told us how to believe, and this is very good for us."

Then a woman stood and said, "Yes, I agree with my colleague. You see, in my country, whenever anyone tells us what to believe, we know he is lying. The harder he pushes, the more we disbelieve him. Your approach is very helpful for us." From that point on, the evening flowed with some of the most honest and perceptive questions I have ever heard about faith.

AN INEFFECTUAL APOLOGETIC

*T*heir comments taught me more about apologetics—the discipline of giving a reasonable and respectful explanation for our faith—than anything I have read or heard elsewhere. Such new insights are needed, because even in the transition period, our old apologetic has been losing effectiveness. I see several reasons for this loss of energy. First, the old apologetic too often resorts to circular reasoning. Second, it is too often defensive, not offensive. Third, it often mistakes potential friends for enemies. Fourth, it is strangely "worldly." Fifth, it tends to get distracted. Sixth, it becomes dishonest when it gets desperate. Let me explain what I mean by each of these factors.

1. Circular Reasoning

When everyone *de facto* believes the Bible, we can afford to prove our points with proof-texts. But as the world changes and more and more people show themselves ignorant or skeptical of the Bible, saying "The Bible says" doesn't prove anything. (Lest you be tempted to quote Isaiah's words about the Word never returning void, remember that Jesus himself told the Pharisees, "You nullify the word of God . . ." [Matthew 15:6; Mark 7:13].)

I believe this is why Paul didn't quote the Bible to the Athenians in Acts 17; he knew that to persuade people, we have to start where they are and build the bridge from their side to ours. So he quoted their poets, not his prophets. And I believe this is why Jesus spoke to the masses in parables. Scandal of scandals: He didn't stick to expository Bible teaching!

The old apologetic was effective when it was helping nominal Christians, who assumed biblical authority, discover a vital faith. It has been losing effectiveness as nominalism (i.e., being Christian in name only) gives way to secularism (i.e., dropping the Christian label as well) and as biblical authority is either questioned or unheard of rather than assumed. On the other side, the Bible serves less as the authoritative foundation for apologetics as a part of the fabric of the message itself.

2. Defensiveness

Our apologetics have been too reactive. In a sense, apologetics waited for evolution to attack and then mustered a defense. It waited for communism to attack, then mustered a defense. It waited for relativism to attack, then mustered a defense. Yet, on those rare occasions when it has sallied forth offensively, it has been surprisingly effective. Consider the writings of a C. S. Lewis or a Flannery O'Connor or a Walker Percy—or even a Fulton Sheen or Robert Schuller or Billy Graham.

3. Combativeness

This defensiveness bred a serious tactical error, repeated on several fronts. We saw our audience not as students or clients but as enemies—not exactly a choice communication strategy! We were like doctors who are furious at their patients for needing help: "Why are you bleeding? You're not supposed to bleed! You should be ashamed of yourself for making this horrible mess."

Not only that, but certain issues were seen as weapons of the enemy when they could just as well have been seen as potential friends instead. Take evolution, for example. What? The theory of evolution as a friend to Christianity? Isn't that unthinkable? Maybe not.

If by the term *evolution* we mean a purely natural, accidental, mindless mechanism that explains the development of everything (including life and consciousness) within an airtight system of physics and chemistry (without God or Spirit or transcending meaning) by impersonal randomness plus time plus nothing—then, of course, we are looking at an irreconcilable enemy to Christianity. In this view, evolution is an uncreated, self-existent, and universal principle or force that "selects" and "leads" toward complexity and even intelligence. It starts to look a lot like a god itself, leaving the position filled and the Christian God standing in the unemployment line with nothing to do. (Not incidentally, this philosophy, or worldview, or anti-religious attitude of evolution has been under significant strain in recent years—a strain imposed not as much by the so-called creation scientists as by mainstream scientists themselves who see huge gaps and problems in Darwinist theory.)

But if by the term *evolution* we mean simply an observation of adaptive development from simple to complex, a pattern of change suggested by the data of the fossil record, then we have something potentially very different. We have one of the possible means by which God created. As such, evolutionary process can be seen not as an enemy of God, or as a god itself, but rather as a creation of God. In this view, it would be a creation intended to produce other creations, a "natural" tool used by a supernatural God, a creative process or tool of God's design (such as erosion or plate tectonics) for producing planet earth as we know it. If evolution is seen in this way, it can become yet another of the praiseworthy elements of the universe's design, inspiring awe and wonder, leading to adoration and worship of the Creator—not denial and disenfranchisement. Behold—an enemy becomes a friend.

We would have been far wiser if our apologists had been less combative when confronting evolution. We could have acknowledged the existence of patterns of change and conceded that maybe (this is just theory, after all) these patterns reveal one of God's mechanisms of creation (along with others such as miracles). Meanwhile, we could have explored the absurdity of a godless evolutionary philosophy: haphazard accidents of evolution mindlessly producing mind, unconsciously producing consciousness, lifelessly producing life, accidentally acting with apparent purpose. C. S. Lewis understood these absurdities,[1] but too few others did, it seems. If we had not overreacted and cast evolution as an enemy, we could have explored a more strategic, irenic approach. Perhaps it's not too late to do so.

4. Worldliness

In the post-Enlightenment age, something was credible because it was written by an "authority" and found in a textbook or, even better, an encyclopedia. So, to enhance our credibility we rested our whole argument on presenting the Bible as a textbook. Never mind that the genre of encyclopedic textbook is a new genre, unheard of in Bible times. Never mind that so much of the Bible is poetry, art—not intended to be read with the wooden style of modern textbooks. Never mind that, as a textbook, the Bible is rather poor, lacking as it is in consistent technical vocabulary, point of view, and so on. We slipped into trying to fit the Bible into the hot genre of the day, and in doing so, I believe, we sold the Bible short. Its real power lies on a much higher level—a level that textbooks can't pretend to touch. So right about the time our culture had tired of the rationalistic textbook approach to learning, we ourselves had forgotten that the Bible might be seen as anything else. What a pity!

5. Distraction

In the process, apologetics got distracted from hunting tigers to chasing field mice. Instead of focusing on the eternal need for God, meaning, values, morals, and moorings, our apologetics focused on fossils, archeology, politics, legislation, and personal problems, especially those of teenagers. And I don't think we were very good at addressing any of these topics. "It's the economy, stupid" was the motto of a recent election campaign; "It's the God-thing, stupid" could have done us a lot of good as a motto, too. "Is there meaning to life?" is a tiger question; "Is the earth ten thousand years old?" is a field mouse question. This is not to eliminate the latter type of question but rather to regain a sense of perspective and priority.

6. Dishonesty

In desperation we started exaggerating our claims, like a frantic salesman on television:

— "Believe in Jesus, and all your diseases will be healed!"
— "Believe now, because the world is going to end next month!"
— "The Bible has *all* the answers to *all* of life's problems!"

These exaggerations were a sign of our desperation. They were false advertising. By overstating the value of what the gospel would do for people, they contradicted it and undersold its ultimate value: that it tells the truth. In so doing, the old apologetic overpromised and underdelivered and thus created a huge pool of dissatisfied customers. Apologetics is tough enough to the secular person; it's even tougher to the burned believer.

FIVE NEW THEMES

So what will the new apologetics look like? I think it will have at least five themes.

1. We don't just offer "answers"; we offer mysteries.

In the twentieth century we felt that offering answers was our best apologetic. Questions such as "Why am I here? Where does life come from? Where am I going? What is my purpose?" will still be essential to the new apologetic. But here is the difference:

In the old apologetic, we acted as if we had easy answers to these questions, as if they were math problems. Our easy answers wore pretty thin pretty fast. In the new apologetic, we offer the faith, not because it has easy answers to the big questions (that is, shallow answers to deep questions), but because the faith is the context in which one can explore the mysteries that underlie these questions. Instead of "Here's the solution to your mathematical problem," we will say "Here's the place to learn math," or better yet, "Here's the place to work with your questions, live your questions, explore possible answers, and find direction to live by."

Another way to say it: A naïve mind thinks that life is a problem to be solved through easy answers. The disillusioned mind, tired of easy answers, thinks life is a paradox to be accepted with willpower (or negatively, with resignation). The seeking mind thinks that behind the superficial problems and apparent paradoxes, life is at heart a mystery to be explored, using faith. In the twenty-first century the new church will feed the seeking mind with the savory mysteries of Creation, Incarnation, Trinity, Atonement, transformation, and unity.

2. We don't debate minutiae; we focus on essentials.

Is there a God? Can God be known or experienced? Can there be any certainty about God, and if so, what kind? What is God like? How should we live if we are believers? How should they search who are unbelievers and also seekers? Why should unbelieving nonseekers consider a change of status? How do we evaluate the various world religions? What are the consequences of not believing anything, or not being sure? What are the benefits of believing? Why so many religions and so many Christian denominations? Why isn't the truth more obvious to more people? It will be to the tiger questions, not the field mouse questions, that the new church will devote her best energies.

3. We don't push credibility alone; we also stress plausibility.

Credibility has to do with the intellectual coherence and verifiable evidence for our faith. Plausibility has to do with its beauty and satisfactions—balanced realistically with its costs and struggles—as it is lived out in real life. If we don't sufficiently stress plausibility, people may concede, "Yes, Christianity has a certain logic; it can be seen to make sense." But, they will quickly add, "It doesn't appeal to me." If we don't sufficiently stress credibility, people may say, "Yes, those Christians are delightful folk, but how can such nice people believe such a load of nonsense?"

Credibility answers the intellectual questions: Is this message logical, intelligent, believable, supported by sufficient evidence? Plausibility explores additional social and emotional questions:

—If this message is credible, could I live with it, and would I want to?

—Would embracing it make me a better person or a worse one?

—Would this contribute to my happiness and health, or to my disintegration and dysfunction?

—What kinds of individuals, communities, and cultures have been produced by this belief heretofore?

—Does the quality of these "fruits" recommend the quality of the "tree" that produced them?

—Can I get along with the people who espouse this belief?

—Would their culture—their music, art, social activities, rules, taboos, practices, rituals, politics—be abhorrent to me, or enjoyable?

—Would I be ashamed to be associated with other believers in this message?

—Can I afford to believe this in terms of my time and monetary resources—can I handle the costs of believing?

—Will what I give to believe this message be compensated by sufficient benefits?

—Can I imagine myself as a bona fide believer, and do I like the picture I imagine?

By taking plausibility questions seriously, we acknowledge that choosing a path for one's life is more than an intellectual choice. Of course, it is not less than intellectual, either. If both issues are critical in choosing one's path, it doesn't matter how well we present one issue; we won't help people reach a point of true commitment until we address the other issue as well.

This linking of credibility and plausibility runs strong through Jesus' teachings. Human beings don't know the truth by abstract logic alone, he suggests, but by experimenting with doing God's will (John 7:17; 8:31–32). The apostle Paul echoes that the proof comes in the practicing (Romans 12:2). So, to stress credibility without plausibility, or plausibility without credibility, would be an insult to our audience—and would dishonor our faith. We fell to one side or the other too often in the late modern world. We will need to walk tall, straight, and sure on the other side.

STRATEGY SIX

4. We don't condemn our competitors; we see them as colleagues of sorts and reason with them with winsome gentleness and respect.

It is a sign of desperation when a disputant has to attack an opponent personally. Yet much of our apologetic has been, in the final analysis, sophisticated (or not so sophisticated) name-calling:

—"That's secular humanism!"
—"You're liberal!"
—"That's pantheism!"

Yes . . . and so?

One of the toughest challenges in the church on the other side will be to develop a new way of talking about—and with—other religions. To dismiss Buddhism when all Buddhists lived on the other side of the world was easy; but when a Buddhist lives next door or teaches your college chemistry class and proves to be a very good neighbor or professor, his or her beliefs are not so easily dismissed. To caricature all Muslims as terrorists is easy until you meet a Muslim of grace and ethical depth. To focus on the cruelties of some Hindus and in so doing dismiss Hinduism might work until a Hindu points out a few of our own embarrassments and egregious failures as Christians. Just as we must acknowledge that both kooks and saints stand under the Christian banner, we will have to stop giving ourselves permission to be prejudiced and stereotypical about members of other religions. We can't keep comparing our best with their worst and feeling smug. (That's a sentence probably worth reading again.)

Dealing with Pluralism's Twin Dangers. If we were living five hundred or even one hundred years ago, chances are we could have misunderstood and misrepresented followers of other religions without risk of rebuttal. Relatively few of us would ever have known a Muslim, a Buddhist, an animist, or even a Jew, so misconceptions and caricatures have free course.

But in today's world, and more so in tomorrow's, we drink coffee, eat lunches, do business, play golf, and cut lawns side by side with members of other religions every day. No longer are they a faceless "they." They are our son's soccer teammate or our daughter's date. They are real people—our neighbors and our friends.

Learning to live with diversity in daily life—one meaning of the word *pluralism*—presents us with new challenges. Will religious debate curdle every social interaction? Or in the name of social etiquette, will we never discuss religion at all and thus forgo evangelism? These are the challenges of a pluralist society.

Pope John Paul II's treatment of pluralism in *Crossing the Threshold of Hope* may offer the church on the other side an example both in tone and apologetic strategy:

> Further along, the Council remarks that "the Catholic Church rejects nothing that is true and holy in these [other] religions." The Church has a high regard for their conduct and way of life, for those precepts and doctrines which, although differing on many points from that which the Church believes and propounds, often reflect a ray of that truth which enlightens all men. However, the Church proclaims, and is bound to proclaim, that Christ is "the way the truth and the life" [John 14:6], in whom men must find the fullness of religious life and in whom God has reconciled everything to Himself (Nostra Aetate 2).
>
> The words of the Council recall the conviction, long rooted in the Tradition, of the existence of the so-called *semina Verbi* (seeds of the Word), present in all religions. In the light of this conviction, the Church seeks to identify the *semina Verbi* present in the great traditions of the Far East, in order to trace a common path against the backdrop of the needs of the contemporary world. . . . The church is guided by the faith that God the Creator wants to save all humankind in Jesus Christ, the only mediator between God and man. . . . In another passage the Council says that the Holy Spirit works effectively even outside the visible structures of the Church (cf. Lumen Gentium 13), making use of these very *semina Verbi*, that constitute a kind of common soteriological root present in all religions.[2]

The pope's approach seeks to avoid twin dangers. On the one hand, he seeks to avoid a divisive, derisive tone. This is essential, because in a world torn by division and hatred, people instinctively feel that a faith that adds to the division, that fuels the hatred, that erects rather than bridges barriers, is part of the problem, not part of the solution. On the other hand, the pope seeks to avoid a relativistic solution. He doesn't say, "Everybody's okay; it doesn't matter what you believe—just believe something."

Why Relativism Fails. Such relativism, though nondivisive, fails for two reasons. First, relativism offers no standard for stopping the crazies: Is it all right for a group of people to bomb buildings in Oklahoma, or poison citizens in train stations in Tokyo, or poison themselves in a commune in Guyana, or oppress women or religious minorities in Saudi Arabia, since doing so is an expression of sincere beliefs that are as valid as anyone else's? Or is there a time and place to say that such a belief is misguided, untrue, and evil? So much for "absolute relativism." Second, relativism tends to trivialize the very beliefs it is trying to promote tolerance for. A relativist begins by saying, "It doesn't really matter *what* you believe," and too often comes to say eventually, "It doesn't really matter *if* you believe."

Counter Strategies to Relativism. The new church must avoid both of these failures of relativism. It can succeed by doing three things. First, the church must present the Christian faith not as one religious army at war against all other religious armies but as one of many religious armies fighting against evil, falsehood, destruction, darkness, and injustice. It respects and values its colleagues in the fight; without their restraining influence on the darker aspects of human nature, this world would be in much more trouble than it is. This is an important distinction and reflects an important shift in tone and strategy. But to stop here would be a partial surrender to relativism.

The second thing, then, is that the church must call people to join a mission, to sign up in the fight against evil—and not only evil out there but also evil in here, in our own hearts and in our own religions. The church must call people from being part of the problem to becoming part of the solution. But the task is not yet finished. Which mission will people join? In a pluralistic world, there are many choices.

So, third, the church must help people decide which mission to join. Contrary to relativism's implications, it does matter which mission one joins. Why join the Christian cause? Why not another? Here is where the new apologetic gets put to work.

If people decide to "suit up" in the Christian cause, the church will have to help them get through spiritual boot camp. But by then, we have moved beyond apologetics and into program.

People are sick of religions fighting with each other (except, of course, some of those doing the fighting!). Most of us don't want to embrace another religion that is peddled by so many cranky people.

However, the religion that can enlist people in a fight with evil—wherever it is found, including in our own hearts and religious communities and systems—that religion will win their hearts. The religion that sees the pride in Pharisees "in here" and the devotion in prostitutes "out there," the religion that hears Satan whispering in the top disciple and that sees love exemplified in a Samaritan wayfarer—that religion will inspire their allegiance. The religion that recognizes its worthlessness if it's all talk and no action (all leaves and no fruit)—that religion will get them out of bed on Sunday morning, and more. The religion that sees true faith wherever it is found—including in an "outsider" from the "wrong" background, such as a Roman centurion or a Syrophoenician woman (see Luke 7:1–10 and Mark 7:24–30)— and not only sees it, but also affirms it, accepts it, commends it, celebrates it—that religion will win them for life. But wait! Aren't we talking about the kingdom of God, proclaimed and demonstrated by Jesus Christ?

5. We don't rush people; we help them at a healthy pace.

Twentieth-century Americans like me were taught to focus on an instant salvation, a decision-oriented regeneration, a conversion event. The church on the other side, more in keeping with Christians throughout history, will emphasize the process of conversion, not only the event. Just as the birth event is the culmination of a long process, and is the commencement of another long process, and in and of itself constitutes a process (and a laborious one at that)—so the conversion event will be seen in the new church as a snapshot of a flowing river, a rain shower in a larger weather system, an important episode in an all-important process.

As a result, we won't rush people toward a decision. We will see rushed decisions as potential abortions—harmful, dangerous, even criminal. We will see this process and its component events as all taking place under the watchful eye of a provident, relational, dynamic God.

A NEW EVANGELISM

*T*his new apologetic really opens into a new evangelism. To my knowledge, no one so far has described this new apologetic and evangelism better than George Hunter in his book *How to Reach Secular People*.[3] Hunter is right, I think, in pointing out how this approach is more like the apologetic and evangelism of the apostolic times even though it is less like the American experience of the nineteenth and twentieth centuries. Specific evangelistic strategies will come and go—including mass evangelism, crusade evangelism, street evangelism, relational evangelism, lifestyle evangelism, sports evangelism, child evangelism, literature evangelism, concert evangelism, church-based evangelism, etc., etc. Beneath these changing evangelistic strategies, this new apologetic will be taking shape, and it will be essential for the church on the other side.

Learn a New Rhetoric

*Realize that old
communication patterns are
less and less effective in the new
world, and discover new,
appropriate modes of discourse.*

Nobody speaks Old High German anymore. Nor does anyone speak King James English. But have we faced the fact that tomorrow's people won't speak our language either?

I am not talking about our lexicon or our grammar, although they will, no doubt, change some, too. Rather, I am referring to our modes of discourse, our ways of arguing, our ways of structuring communications. I am referring to what makes a message boring or interesting, cogent or unconvincing, moving or cold, motivating or repulsive, funny or trite, overstated or understated, in good taste or in bad, delightful or ponderous.

Will our words and concepts and methods of communication from the old world still work on the other side? Will the words and concepts derived from old-world experience be like Confederate money on the other side of the Civil War? Will we need a new currency of thought and discourse to communicate in and as the church on the other side? Will our discourse be fighting words, or propaganda, or technical discourse, or poetry? I have five hunches in this regard. Whether my hunches are right or wrong, they suggest a fact that is hard to dispute: On the other side, if we want to communicate, we will need to learn a new rhetoric. Dietrich Bonhoeffer was onto this need decades ago—perhaps not surprisingly, since he himself was plunged into a new world the likes of which had not been seen before.

> Reconciliation and redemption, regeneration and the Holy Spirit, love of our enemies, cross and resurrection, life in Christ and Christian discipleship—all these things are so difficult and so remote that we hardly venture any more to speak of them. In the traditional words and acts we suspect that there may be something quite new and revolutionary, though we cannot as yet grasp or express it. That is our own fault. Our church, which has been fighting in these years only for its self-preservation, as though that were an end in itself, is incapable of taking the work of reconciliation and redemption to mankind and the world. Our earlier words are therefore bound to lose their force and cease, and our being Christians today will be limited to two things: prayer and righteous action among men. . . .
>
> It is not for us to prophesy the day (though the day will come) when men will once more be called so to utter the word of God that the world will be changed and renewed by it. It will be a new language, perhaps quite non-religious, but liberating and redeeming—as was Jesus' language; it will shock people and yet overcome them by its power; it will be the language of a new righteousness and truth, proclaiming God's peace with men and the coming of his kingdom. . . . Till then the Christian cause will be a silent and hidden affair, but there will be those who pray and do right and wait for God's own time.[1]

FIVE HUNCHES ABOUT A NEW RHETORIC

1. In the reinvented church on the other side, our words will not stand alone. Our message will be a life: words plus deeds. Words of faith without works of love will not survive; no one will listen. A rhetoric of integrity—words integrated with deeds—will carry the day. Was it St. Francis who reputedly said to his young trainees, "Everywhere you go, preach the gospel, and when it is absolutely necessary, use words"? Such instruction will be well appreciated on the other side. There our churches may be evaluated as much by their menus of short-term mission options as by their doctrinal statements, because the deeds will matter as much as the words.

Some will fear this condition, seeing yet more evidence of "dumbing down." Others will celebrate it as the reconnection of tree and fruit that Jesus described, or the faith with works that James demanded. Feared or celebrated, it marks an important element of rhetoric in the new church.

2. Words of truth will not be less important, but they will be fewer and simpler and softer if they are to have power. We now suffer from a glut of words, trumpeted loudly. To be listened to on the other side, we must learn to whisper short secrets.

3. Our words will seek to be servants of mystery, not removers of it as they were in the old world. They will convey a message that is clear yet mysterious, simple yet mysterious, substantial yet mysterious. My faith developed in the old world of many words, in a naïve confidence in the power of many words, as if the mysteries of faith could be captured like fine-print conditions in a legal document and reduced to safe equations. Mysteries, however, can not be captured so precisely. Freeze-dried coffee, butterflies on pins, and frogs in formaldehyde all lose something in our attempts at capturing, defining, preserving, and rendering them less jumpy, flighty, or fluid. In the new world, we will understand this a little better.

4. Our words will be less religious, more common, more earthy. Religious jargon and allusions that assume prior "insider" knowledge—such as my reference to Balaam in chapter 4—will be "out": extra baggage, too-high hurdles, stones in the shoes of the new world's spiritual travelers. We will speak less evangelicalese and more plain English (or Spanish or Chinese or whatever).

Don't worry, my fellow liberal arts majors, for the new world will be a highly educated world (though perhaps less reliant on printed media?), so our diction can have much to offer intelligent readers. But in a world of such diversity, the days of Ebenezers raised where angels prostrate fall, with second blessings upon royal diadems in Zion, with a thousand tongues lifting up ineffable epiphanies on high unto the seventh heavens—those days will probably be long gone. The change to a more earthy, human diction will be good for us. The discipline of thinking clearly, feeling honestly, saying what we mean and meaning what we say—that's a discipline our souls need. For followers of Jesus, that discipline will make us more like our Leader.

5. Our rhetoric will depend more on the power of story. In this way, the church on the other side will be more like the world of Jesus and the Bible—more Eastern (Middle Eastern, to be exact), a meeting point between left and right brains, integrating objective and subjective, analytical (taking apart) and synthetic (putting together).

So, in the new world, believers telling their neighbors the good news will still use words, and with great care. But they will know that their words must be the tip of the iceberg, buoyed by a life lived well with laughter, love, compassion, and generosity. Preachers will use words with great care, also—being careful never to bore, not to overstate or overpromise, not to dishonor logic or truth or integrity or creativity. They will seek to convey mystery, but not to mystify. The mentor will use words—but only a few, and only after much listening to both the protégé and the Spirit of God. The theologian will use words, but like Jesus, he will be a weaver of parables, a designer of proverbs, more a sage than a technician.

Christians will use words less flippantly, more like lovers and artists and less like lawyers and salesmen. We deal with precious meanings, with love stories, with antidotes and cures that can save lives but can become poisons if they are not prepared with care. Syllogism and story, classification and metaphor, cause-effect and allegory, rhetoric and poetry, understatement and wild exaggeration for effect—our rhetoric will reflect our increased sensitivity to words and their vast and varied potential for changing people.

Interestingly, here in the transition zone we are already seeing signs of the other side. More and more authors indulge in both nonfiction and fiction, both parable and propositions. Our best teachers do not just lecture, but also tell wonderful stories. Twenty centuries of Christian literature will teach us something about what kinds of words and discourse last and carry and echo over time—which kinds

STRATEGY SEVEN

clarify, edify, make for peace, or stir schism. Like Paul, we will beg for others to pray for us, simply that we may speak clearly, as we ought to (Colossians 4).

SPEAKING OF RELIGION . . .

*T*he highlight of my higher education was my master's thesis. I was fortunate enough to stumble onto an American novelist, Walker Percy, while he was still living. Equally fortunate, I stumbled onto his closest literary confidante, Lewis Lawson, who was a professor at my university. I was able to correspond with Percy and meet him. Among my most prized possessions are two letters he wrote me, which I have framed for my office wall.

Percy became a Christian the hard way. His parents died while he was a teenager, at least one of them by suicide. He was then raised by an eccentric, intellectual uncle. After medical school, as an intern preparing to practice pathology, he contracted pulmonary tuberculosis from a cadaver and went to a sanatorium in the Adirondacks for "the cure"—rest and fresh air. While he was there, contemplating the possibility of death, he began reading literature. First came the existentialists—Sartre, Camus, then Kierkegaard, to whom the existentialists kept referring—then Thomas Aquinas and the Bible.

Percy recovered, but he never practiced medicine. He became a novelist—a secret-agent evangelist, if you will—trying to help others find God through the medium that was used to bring him to faith.

Consider his thoughts on the delicate process of speaking about religion. (Wherever he used the word *novelist*, I suggest substituting the word *communicator.*)

> The American Christian novelist faces a peculiar dilemma today. (I speak, of course, of a dilemma of the times and not of his own personal malaise, neuroses, failures, to which he is at least as subject as his good heathen colleagues, sometimes I think more so.) His dilemma is that though he professes a belief which he holds saves himself and the world

and nourishes his art besides, it is also true that Christendom seems in some sense to have failed. Its vocabulary is worn out. This twin failure raises problems for a man who is a Christian and whose trade is with words. . . .

The Christian novelist is like a man who goes to a wild lonely place to discover the truth within himself and there after much ordeal and suffering meets an apostle who has the authority to tell him a great piece of news and so tells him the news with authority. He, the novelist, believes the news and runs back to the city to tell his countrymen, only to discover that the news has already been broadcast, that this news is in fact the weariest canned spot announcement on radio-TV, more commonplace than the Exxon commercial, that in fact he might just as well be shouting Exxon! Exxon! for all anyone pays any attention to him.[2]

What, then, is the Christian communicator—who has "cast his lot with a discredited Christendom and having inherited a defunct vocabulary"—to do in these circumstances? Percy suggests two tactics. First, the Christian communicator, calling on "every ounce of cunning, craft, and guile he can muster from the darker regions of his soul," must be willing to reach for the bizarre, the shocking, the comic. Percy refers to fellow Catholic novelist Flannery O'Connor in this regard, who responded to a query about the bizarre quality of her fictional characters with this maxim: If you are drawing for nearly blind people, you must draw caricatures—large ones, simple ones, exaggerated ones. Interestingly, the great Catholic theologian Romano Guardini reached the same conclusion as these two Catholic novelists, but for a different reason. Rather than by the condition of his audience, the Christian communicator is driven to the same approach by the very nature of his subject matter. Guardini says:

> When a human being in the grip of divine power attempts to convey something of God's holy "otherness" he tries one earthly simile after another. In the end he discards them all as inadequate and says apparently wild and senseless things meant to startle the heart into feeling what lies beyond the

STRATEGY SEVEN

reaches of the brain. Something of the kind takes place here: "Eye has not seen nor ear heard, nor has it entered into the heart of man, what things God has prepared for those who love him" (I Cor. 2:9). They can be brought closer only by the overthrow of everything naturally comprehensible. Flung into a world of new logic, we are forced to make a genuine effort to understand.[3]

Percy's second tactic echoes Bonhoeffer's strategy of silence, recalled at the beginning of this chapter. Sometimes the best way to be heard above the din of "Exxon! Exxon!" (and ringing doorbells) is simply to speak less:

> . . . in these times everyone is an apostle of sorts, ringing doorbells and bidding his neighbor to believe this and do that. In such times, when everyone is saying "Come!" when radio and television say nothing else but "Come!" it may be that the best way to say "Come!" is to remain silent. Sometimes silence itself is a "Come!"[4]

And having said that, I have probably said enough.

8

Abandon Structures as They Are Outgrown

*Adopt a new paradigm for church
structure that allows
for routine reengineering based on
changes in size, constituency,
resources, and strategy.*

*I*f you are a member or a leader of a church of 150 people, you probably have an ecclesiology—a theology of the church, a paradigm for church structure—that suits that size. If you transfer to a church of 1,500 people, even in the same denomination, you will encounter a different ecclesiology, because churches of different sizes view themselves differently.

Two things that are exceedingly difficult to change in this world are the size of a church—in the direction of larger, that is—and the theology of a church. The only thing harder than changing both of them at the same time is trying to change the first without changing the second.

The transition-zone phenomenon called the Church Growth Movement provided more than adequate proof of this maxim. Armed with seminars, books, tapes, subscriptions, and consultations, the movement tried to assault the inertia of most churches in regard to growth. Sadly, ecclesiology too often thwarted the best of intentions. Good church-growth programs would be rendered as powerless as Superman by kryptonite when confronted with a small-church ecclesiology. In the new world, a new ecclesiology will develop that can fit churches of various sizes and that can actually encourage rather than obstruct church growth.

A SYMPHONY WITHOUT A SCORE

Take, for example, a church with an anarchist ecclesiology. (Don't laugh—it's more common than you think.) This ecclesiology sees problems in "the institutional church" (which is another term for "the church wherever it actually exists") and concludes that they result from its being "organized." According to this way of thinking, the early church was blissfully spontaneous. The Holy Spirit led individuals with such power and mastery that the early church performed like a symphony without a score. The beautiful music poured out harmoniously from the untrained musicians as they were moved extemporaneously by the Invisible Conductor.

Never mind that no one has ever actually seen a church like this function for very long, or that when a church appears to so function, it turns out to be the product of covert human leadership and training from a real-though-unwritten rule book. Never mind that the whole second half of the New Testament seems to be about problems arising in the early church, with organized yet Spirit-inspired solutions being developed to deal with them. Never mind that organization is a fact of life for every organism—from paramecia to blue whales. Never mind, because some good folk in every generation are going to try to start churches that operate with as little overt organization as possible, fighting organization with at least as much zeal as they use in fighting sin.

Despite these words of criticism, I call these anti-organizationalists "good folk" with good reason, and not only because I was once one of them. They are idealists, and their idealism is attractive. They are driven to work hard and love long and bleed deep for their dream of building a community unspoiled by institutionalism and organization. And I wholeheartedly concur that organization and institutionalism can obstruct community as effectively as telephone wires can ruin a beautiful view. I sent one of these "good folk," a most enjoyable friend, a copy of this manuscript, and he replied,

> I read your unfinished manuscript twice. . . . My experience tells
> me that [real Christianity] won't work in the institutional

church no matter what side. The truth, as I see it, is that the visible and the physical work against the invisible and spiritual. . . . If God is leading you to write this book, I am in your corner. However, in my heart, I just don't think "the church on the other side" will ever exist.

My friend is working out his perspective by lowering his expectations of the institutional church to near zero, focusing instead on interpersonal relationships—"loving my neighbors," as he would say. And I don't quarrel with him; I like what he is doing. But the fact is, if some well-meaning people like my friend, wary of the side effects of organization, gather regularly as friends in a home or a restaurant—not in an elaborate "church" building— forming a group that thrives on unstructured relationships with no formal leadership and as little as possible of the dreaded "O-word"—then one of four things will happen:

- The little proto-church will thrive for many years as a small circle of friends requiring very little organization, perhaps aided by the fact that (1) they don't call themselves a church, and (2) they don't invite too many people to join them.
- The little church will die after a few months or perhaps a few years.
- The little church will adopt a "cell church model," dividing in two as soon as the size of the group requires organization, thus increasing in numbers by multiplying small groups. However, if this works long-term (which seems to happen less in reality than in theory), they will soon discover that they are indeed organized—just differently—and that the organizational demands of keeping a cell-multiplication movement going (such as leadership training or problem solving) can equal or surpass those of a more traditional church.
- The little church will grow, change its ecclesiology—with agony, of course—and get organized. In the process of changing its ecclesiology, many late-night discussions will take place featuring heated debates that rival Luther's at Leipzig.

More than likely, this group, if it capitulates to organization, will enfranchise an ecclesiology that will allow the fledgling church to grow from, say, 40 to 150. At this level, the following structural elements will be typical:

- One pastor—volunteer, bivocational, or salaried
- A formal or informal board that serves as the volunteer staff of the church, attending to administration and ministry

At about 150, a church that wishes to keep growing will probably hire a second pastoral staff member. This move is far more monumental than it seems, for at least four reasons:

- The pastor, who may have excelled with volunteers, now may be asked to supervise the second staff person. Managing staff requires skills that are in many ways antithetical to those previously required with volunteers. Few people are good at both. If neither pastor is seen as the chief of staff, the church will generally slide into another slick of risks and problems, ranging from ineffectiveness due to a lack of accountability to ineffectiveness due to power struggles.
- The board must give up some of its power to this new staff person. It is human nature not to give up power without a struggle unless those who hold it are thoroughly exhausted and tired of the responsibility that comes with their authority.
- The second staff person, besides dealing with an inexperienced pastor and an ambivalent board, is working for a church that can barely afford to pay a salary and has little patience with setbacks or delays in productivity. To make matters worse, this person generally joins the staff with high ideals, boundless goodwill, and a bit of naïveté. He may also bring any number of his own needs or pathologies to the situation—seeing the pastor as a father-figure, ministry as a way to be liked, associate-pastor status as a means to power without responsibility, or some other image.
- The congregation, with many idealists from the first stage, welcome the new staff person and fear him at the same

time. Will this person compete with their beloved pastor (or, conversely, will this person compensate for the pastor they secretly distrust)? Will this person change the homey church they love by making it more "corporate" (i.e., organized)? Their unspoken mandate—an impossible assignment if ever there was one—is this: Help our church grow, but don't you dare change it.

If the church survives this structural transition, it will more than likely grow toward numbers between 300 and 800, but another ceiling awaits it there. This ceiling results from some or all of the following:

- As additional staff are hired, the now-senior pastor's role changes: less ministry, more leadership, more staff management, more administration. Few pastors can survive a change in role of this magnitude.
- The additional staff hired at these early stages are nearly always generalists, or at least multitalented. A music director, for example, may also direct Christian education or small groups. But with growth in numbers comes greater demand for specialization. A "B+" musician who is also a "B+" Christian education director was a godsend to the church of 250; she may be an embarrassment to the church of 600 that wants—and can now afford—"A"-caliber staff in both categories. To put it bluntly, the same staff that helped the church surmount the earlier ceiling can create this one by being good in general but not good enough in specialized areas.
- A fully staffed church no longer needs the board that helped create it. In place of volunteer administrators or unpaid pastors, it now needs a board that does one or both of the following: (1) provides oversight in a way more akin to a nonprofit board of directors, skilled in strategic planning, oversight, organizational management, budgeting, and whenever possible, fund-raising; and (2) functions as spiritual mentors, perhaps as resident mystics, devoted to intercessory prayer, exemplifying and

conserving the organization's values, history, and accumulated wisdom, attuned to matters of the Spirit, and thus constituting the organization's soul.

- Put the three previous elements together, and you basically guarantee a time of internal conflict:

  —The pastor is frustrated with the staff he hired a few years ago, because their skill levels in specific areas now seem deficient.

  —The staff members are frustrated with their senior pastor, who used to be satisfied with them but now, for some reason unknown to them, is not.

  —The pastor and staff are frustrated with the very board that sets their salaries and has such devotion to the church, because this board either micromanages or becomes obstructionistic—which it does in an understandable attempt to assert itself for some useful purpose in its new and unfamiliar role.

  —The board is frustrated with the pastor and staff, all of whom seem stressed out and less effective because of everything we have already considered.

A famous essay, "Evolution and Revolution as Organizations Grow," describes a cyclical pattern of centralization/crisis/decentralization/crisis that fits this church scenario all too perfectly. Sadly, at each turn of the cycle, good people who love God and at least *used* to love each other find themselves angry, at odds, disappointed in and disappointing one another. Even worse, their Bibles and theology—specifically, their ecclesiology—rather than helping them understand and cope with these natural transitions, seem to get them more and more stuck, not more and more liberated.[1]

ARE THERE SOLUTIONS?

On the other side, surrounded by a world more accustomed to organizational reengineering, divestitures, mergers, buyouts, and sell-offs, the church will develop a more open, stage-oriented ecclesiology. Instead of painting itself into a corner by enfranchising one ecclesiology—which fits it now but won't later on—the church will endow options through a broader, more flexible, multistage paradigm. This ecclesiology, rather than offering a single structural blueprint, will offer some general principles for church structure, all based on one elegant assumption. This assumption is stated succinctly by Kirbyjon Caldwell, as quoted by William Easum: "Organizational structure is like a pair of shoes. You fit the shoes to the feet; you don't make the feet fit the shoes."[2]

The general principles of this new ecclesiology will lead to several conclusions:

1. Whenever good people (who previously got along well and loved one another warmly) start fighting and acting badly, it is probably a sign that the structure is no longer adequate. The interpersonal struggles are symptoms of a structural or systemic problem. Therefore, it is unwise to spiritualize the conflict or demonize the opposition.

2. A structure that works tends to promote growth, which will eventually make the structure obsolete. In other words, yesterday's successes and progress guarantee today's organizational failures and problems. Success today guarantees trouble tomorrow. Churches, like snakes and lobsters, need to shed their organizational skins as they grow.

3. Every trade-up in structure requires someone to give up power or freedom, which in turn entails pain and requires grace and humility. That is, wherever new life flourishes, someone is or has been dying or in some way experiencing "labor pains."

4. Rather than making organization obsolete or superfluous, the Holy Spirit is our resource and guide in how to use, discard, replace, and reengineer structures. The Holy Spirit doesn't mandate new wine in old skins—which no longer stretch to fulfill their purpose—or new wine in no skins, but rather new wine in new skins.[3]

5. The Bible, rather than imposing one perfect structure (such as patriarchy, polygamy, or kingdom), presents a variety of structures through which God works at various times, according to the need of the moment. Scripture therefore demonstrates the need for ongoing organizational evolution—or revolution.

6. The Bible further calls us to seek wisdom, which is another term for "the ability to decide when structures should be preserved and protected, and when they should be adapted or replaced."

7. Smaller churches, instead of feeling superior to large churches because they don't have the same organizational struggles, should instead pay attention and humbly learn from their larger siblings' mistakes, struggles, and successes. There, by the grace of God, they too will go someday. After all, eight-year-old girls have no business feeling smug that they are exempt from the problems of their pubescent big sisters, nor do forty-year-olds when they compare themselves with their aging parents. (The converse is also true, by the way, since every large church of centuries past has, sooner or later, declined to smallness. Instead of feeling smug about their large size, they may have a lot to learn from smaller churches—about economy of scale, sustainability, flexibility, personal nurture, humane values, and potluck dinners, for example.)

Sufficient to the size are the problems thereof, so churches of whatever size should focus on the beam of their own structural problems rather than the splinters of other churches.

8. Every newly forming church should probably plan on restructuring every time it doubles in size, and the congregation should probably bring in experienced, objective, outside consultants more often than they think necessary. When they write their bylaws, they should anticipate these needs for change and facilitate rather than obstruct structural change in their legal documents. They should remind themselves every year that constant change is here to stay and that if their current structures work well, they will necessarily become obsolete.

9. It will often be the case that structures are like cocoons or wombs: They must be left behind before the next stage of development can begin. In other words, a church needs to abandon some structures before they feel the need to do so. They will only know in retrospect—as they spread their wings or breathe fresh air—just how much the change was needed and what they would have missed by postponing the change.

10. A healthy church must balance the need to conserve expertise (by valuing seniority, tenure, and past contribution) with

the need for fresh blood and new ideas. Both time-tested expertise and energetic innovation are needed in times of rapid and radical change. Without the former, huge quantities of energy, time, and money are wasted. The wheel is repeatedly reinvented, the *Titanic* and the *Challenger* are repeatedly and tragically rebuilt and relaunched, Trojan horses are welcomed into the city again and again, and the Alamo is forgotten. Without the advantage of wise and experienced counsel, creative genius shows an amazing proclivity to find ingenious new ways of making the same old foolish mistakes.

But age-old experience itself teaches us that without the fresh, invigorating blood of creativity, organizations drift and descend relentlessly toward plodding gerontocracy, nostalgia, irrelevance, arthritic inflexibility, senility, and death. How sadly rare it is for the older Pauls to enfranchise and encourage the younger Timothies (cf. 1 Timothy 4:12)! How sadly common it is for the young Rehoboams to ignore the counsel of their experienced elders (cf. 2 Chronicles 10)!

No doubt, these twin follies of the old and young will persist in the new world on the other side, with the same sad results. But wise leaders—who themselves follow a Leader who is at once the Ancient of Days and the Young Carpenter never older than thirty-three—will do well to bias their structures toward both conserving expertise and welcoming fresh blood. For example, by having term limits for governing board members, and by moving "retired" governing board members onto advisory boards, organizations can push themselves to bring in new leaders while not losing the expertise of experienced leaders. And just as we train governing boards in management techniques, so we must train advisory boards in the delicate art of advising—an underrated and under-exploited art, one that is sorely needed these days.

11. Structural roles in the church on the other side will be designed with personality theory (or the related concept of spiritual gifts) in mind. For example, if a role requires someone to be at once highly visionary and highly attentive to detail, or to be both a risk taker and a cautionary, or to be both sensitive and tough, or to be equal parts patient and results-oriented, it is almost guaranteed to fit no one well. The role will chafe and wear on

whoever tries to fill it and leave each successive person feeling and looking like a failure. Structures won't work when the roles they create don't match how people are actually wired; neither do they work when the roles change, whether quickly or gradually.

Myers-Briggs and other personality theories have important implications for church structure. Sometimes the choice is this simple: Do we want to save the person in a certain role and change the structure, or keep the structure even though it will cost us the person (through a firing, a resignation, a nervous breakdown, or burnout)? These choices aren't easy, but they will become clearer when we have appropriate sensitivity to roles and personality theory.

12. For all we have said about it, size is only one of the many internal conditions that can produce change and make structural evolution or revolution necessary. Other factors can include changes in constituency (the congregation becomes on average older or younger or richer or poorer, or more or less educated, or more or less employed), commitment, vision or goals, degree of unity, or level of spiritual maturity. With any number of changes afoot, it is easy to make mistakes in the new church, just as it was in the old church.

13. Writing things down can really help. Computer software comes with documentation. Cars come with an owner's manual. Pets come with care information. But how many church roles and structures come with written guidelines, training, instructions, and documentation? What would happen if all church volunteers (not to mention paid staff) went on strike until they had short, basic, written job descriptions? What would happen if all volunteers participated in an annual or biannual evaluation—of themselves, of the structure around them, of the support and training they receive, of their job descriptions? What would happen if this paperwork were kept simple and at a minimum, with a general mission statement, a few key goals, terms of service, clear lines of authority, a description of what success looks like, and evaluation procedures? Would these developments seem too corporate, or would they be examples of doing for others what we wish for ourselves: the maximum opportunity to succeed in our work in the church?

14. Control is less important than catalyzing positive action. William Easum distinguishes control structures from permission-giving structures: "The top-down oppressive approach of bureaucracy is on its way out. In its place are emerging permission-giving networks. These networks are freeing and empowering people to explore their spiritual gifts individually and in teams on behalf of the Body of Christ."[4]

We make an ironic biblical error in this regard. We read, for example, of the problems of the Corinthian church, so we try to exert control to be sure those problems never arise among us. We think this makes us biblical Christians. But in doing this, we guarantee that we will never become the kind of vibrant, exciting, energetic biblical organization that by its nature becomes vulnerable to such problems. Having control is pretty boring when nothing is happening. It is much better to have structures that first encourage something to happen! Envy those who have so much happening that they are legitimately worried about things getting out of control! The question in the new church will not be, How can our structures control, but How can they be catalytic?

15. We need an ecclesiology that acknowledges latent periods without guilt. We are prone to guilt-tripping ourselves and others even though guilt trips take us nowhere but backward. For example, we glorify extraordinary revival experiences so as to feel like failures during ordinary times, not realizing that if last year's extraordinary revival experience continues for more than a few weeks, it becomes the new ordinary experience. If last week's worship was awe inspiring, this week's must at least equal it in emotional force; otherwise, someone is sure to tell us we are backsliding and will threaten to go down the street "where God is really moving." The result in some churches is an ever-inflating hype, which might seem exciting from the outside, but from the inside is pressured, desperate, and pathetic.

The fact is, down times are important for many reasons, not the least of which is that without them there are no up times. All of life runs with times and seasons, ebbs and flows, work and rest, expansion and consolidation, death and birth. This is normal; it is also biblical, and our ecclesiology should acknowledge it.

16. We need an ecclesiology that is streamlined, simple, and less exhausting and time consuming. When we keep adding program to program, never practicing strategic abandonment, we run ourselves ragged and finally despise the church for burning us out. Sometimes we need to admit that we are making the Christian life harder, not easier, through the complex and demanding structures we have created. We need to listen to the "anarchists," like my friend, who are aware of how the visible and physical can work against the invisible and spiritual. We need to go back to the drawing board and conceive of new approaches to structuring church life. Ed Simon calls them "organizational architectures."

> We need a new generation of organizational architects. But to get there we must first correct basic misunderstandings. . . . It's not just rearranging the organization structure. We have to . . . design for the long term—based on understanding interdependencies. Most changes in organization structure are piecemeal reactions to problems. Real designers are continually trying to understand wholes.[5]

It has been said that the church need not be run like a business. It has been better said that the church shouldn't be run like a bad business. It may be even better said that the best businesses and the best churches alike will be "learning organizations," as Peter Senge calls them in *The Fifth Discipline*. As churches learn, they will continually evaluate, fine-tune, adjust, and—when necessary—revolutionize their organization and themselves.

THE MUTATING GENE

*F*aith, hope, and love remain in this life, but not much else, it seems. Sometimes being part of a church feels like playing a game that keeps "morphing" into another game—first Scrabble, then Monopoly, then chess, then Nintendo. The behaviors that scored and won me points last year now draw boos and angry letters or blank stares.

Without knowing even the basics of structure suggested in this chapter, I have gotten down on myself, gotten down on my staff, watched my staff get down on me, and ditto with my board—not once, but many times. It's not a pretty picture. Now that I have gained a little more savvy—sadly, the hard way—I am at least a little more gracious, a little slower to blame others, a little more alert to see people trying to do the best they can in difficult situations.

I used to think I could find the perfect structure for my church, the right balance of power, terms of service, checks and balances, and so on. But now I realize that the perfect structure is just about any that is flexible enough to become a better structure tomorrow. Conversely, the "perfect structure" that claims to be *the* right one, immune to improvement, is actually one of the worst structures possible.

My search for the perfect church structure was about as promising as the search for a perfect pair of pants or shoes that my children would never outgrow. It is clear to me now that in the same way our closets are full of outgrown clothes, so our church files should be full of outgrown structural diagrams. Those diagrams were not failures; they fulfilled their purpose for their time. We should not feel bad for not "getting it right the first time" any more than we feel bad at having to replace worn-out or undersized clothes. Now this all seems pretty obvious, but that kind of insight comes amazingly hard and slowly for many of us.

The next time you are talking about the need for change in your church structure, get your people to consider a bigger change than they had bargained for. Make it not just a change to a different structure, but a change to a different way of thinking about structures. This may be harder to accept in the short run, but it proves to be so much better over time.

9

Save the Leaders

*Recognize the terrible
toll that the transition time
is taking on leaders; recognize
their immense value to the
church at this time; help
them be "saved" for
their needed work.*

Robert Bly begins his book *Iron John* with these words: "We are living at an important and fruitful moment now, for it is clear to men that the images of adult manhood given by the popular culture are worn out; a man can no longer depend on them. By the time a man is thirty-five he knows that the images of the right man, the tough man, the true man which he received in high school do not work in life. Such a man is open to new visions of what a man is or could be."[1]

We could begin a discussion of professional leadership in the new church the same way: "We are living at an important and fruitful moment right now, for it is clear to church leaders that the images of Christian leadership given by the religious subculture are worn out; a minister can no longer depend on them. By the time a person in professional ministry reaches thirty-five, he or she knows that the images of the knowledgeable, doctrinally sound, politically correct, and above all successful pastor that were learned in seminary (and at the Christian bookstore or leadership conference) simply do not work in life. Such a Christian leader is open to new visions of what a Christian and a church leader is or could be."

Here, in the transition zone, it doesn't really matter which leadership model you choose to follow. Before long, you realize that riding that model is like surfing on a two-by-four, or driving an old gas guzzler with a flatulent muffler, or cycling with flat tires and bent rims. Yet these models seemed to work in the old church.

A POPULAR MODEL

Take the know-it-all-Bible-answer-man model, for example. (I have in mind a general stereotype here, not a specific radio personality.) This is the leader who led by knowledge, who made life sound so simple if you merely live by "biblical principles." He could show you why the charismatics (or noncharismatics) or liberals (or legalists) or social activists (or pietists) were wrong and why his "us" was right. For him, there was a simple formula for everything, whether it was finding God's will, getting God to perform a miracle for you, or resolving the mystery of human suffering or the conundrum of human responsibility and divine sovereignty.

Like the secular scientist, this type of leader in the old church gained power through esoteric knowledge. The mystification of his pulpit was really a variation on the scientific laboratory theme. Like the scientist, this church leader often promised to remove mystery through research, leaving only clean doctrines and sterile principles where there once were questions, pain, wonder, and longing. Think of it—demystified principles and doctrines, even less interesting than microscope slides or pickled lab specimens! Through his esoteric techniques (performed in the study, not the lab, and with Greek and Hebrew, not test tubes), he promised to tame the wildness of his subjects—God and life—through late-Industrial Age know-how. But imagine: Taming God! And life! Meanwhile, both subjects stubbornly refused domestication and demystification. So in recent years the unwarranted promise of omniscience and omnipotence became even less attractive in men of the cloth than it had been in men of the lab coat.

Of course, our disillusionment with the Bible-answer-man vision is ambivalent. All of us—I included—wish that the old stereotype had been at least partly true. Life would be so much

STRATEGY NINE

easier, God so much safer, the Bible so much tidier, and Christianity so much easier. But in our postmodern world, most of us have come to realize that God, the Bible, life, and Christianity— like Heisenberg's particles—are wild nonconformists. And we distrust anyone who tries to prove otherwise.

SUCCESS!

*E*nter the next model of leadership: the "successful model." The word *model* itself is interesting enough in this light. We envision a retouched magazine glossy or a pretty person standing by the letters of a television game show or, better yet, the plastic airplane you glued together when you were a kid. Follow the instructions, imitate the picture on the front of the box, and you will be "successful." I can smell the glue even as I write.

Not that I'm against success. The fact is, I care a lot about it, probably too much. But my biggest complaint with the "success" models is that we are almost certain not to succeed by obediently (but mindlessly) imitating them. There are at least four reasons for this ironic condition.

Why Imitating Success Can Guarantee Failure

1. The most celebrated and notoriously successful models of recent decades—Bill Hybels, Rick Warren, and John Maxwell, for example—became successful through bold innovation and creative synthesis, not through unthinking imitation. Thus we can imitate their product, but in so doing, violate the very process that made them successful.

2. The successful models became successful by trying new ideas that were too radical to be popular. Wait until a model is popular enough to imitate and you're almost sure to be too late. Tomorrow's successes are more likely to be considered radical and unpopular today.

3. The truly successful models earned their success the old-fashioned way—through pain, tears, endurance, mistakes, and prayer. (The leaders I have mentioned have done us a wonderful service by being refreshingly honest about their struggles.) In the process,

they developed the very character that made them worthy from God's perspective (I imagine) to be entrusted with something as dangerous, potentially destructive, and burdensome as success. Some of us imitators may be looking for a shortcut—which, as you can see, is not too good an indicator of future success.

4. These "successful models," then, shouldn't really be seen as models at all, not of the pretty-face-on-the-TV type or of the plastic-and-glue type. Instead, they should be seen as real people who have stuck to their dreams and integrity through sweat and tears, have grown up, and have surprised themselves as much as anyone else by their success. For them, remember, success was a risk, an untried dream, not somebody else's formula for success. If you imitate them as successful models, whatever kind of success you get probably won't be the kind they got. The writer to the Hebrews didn't say, "Consider your leaders and imitate their hair styles, speech patterns, and gestures." He said, "Imitate their faith" (Hebrews 13:7).

A New Breed of Leaders

So what can be said about the new breed of leaders needed on the other side? I see at least seven things.

1. Personal authenticity will be characteristic of this new breed of leaders.

Only Bill Hybels can authentically be Bill Hybels, and Billy Graham, Billy Graham. Clones look a little like Elvis impersonators after a while—a curiosity, but not leaders any more than the impersonators are automatically creative musical artists. If leadership by knowledge worked in the old church (or leadership by politics or credentials or charisma or imitation or formula), old approaches will work no longer; on the other side, there will be only leadership by personal authenticity, leadership that flows from who you really are.

Leaders will first have to take inventory of who they are, with or without the various tools that exist to help in the process: thinker or feeler? introvert or extrovert? sensory or intuitive? judgment oriented or perception oriented? dominant, influencing, steady, or compliant? melancholic, choleric, phlegmatic, or sanguine? firstborn, middle, last-born, or only child? left-brained or right-brained? creative, creative-developer, developer, maximizer, etc., etc.?

Then leaders will have to look at the tasks and qualities demanded of them—planning, intercepting entropy, casting vision, aligning resources, troubleshooting, teaching, recruiting, dialoguing.

After that, they will have to realize that they are not equipped to do all that is demanded of them. Nor is anyone else. (At this point, they will have to convince themselves not to quit and go do something else.) This fact points to a second characteristic.

2. Team development will be required of these leaders.

Having faced their own limitations, the leaders will have to design a plan for leveraging what they can do and who they can be by creating teams to help with what they can't do and be. Leadership happens through teams of people being who they are and doing what they are gifted to do. Leading has always been difficult, but leading without awareness of who you are, without teaming with people who similarly know who they are, will be a flat impossibility in the reinvented church.

George Hunter was asked in an interview what he wished he could add to his already very helpful book *Church for the Unchurched*. He addressed this issue of team leadership:

> I would have included something about leadership. . . . Leadership in these churches is team leadership and most pastors are unskilled in this approach and yet it is much more fun. This is the way these churches have solved the problem of succession. . . . The church is much less likely to crater if the pastor leaves because the pastor is one member of a team. Many of these new leaders learned these skills playing soccer, not baseball.[2]

To expand on Hunter's sports analogy, we could say that leaders on the other side will not create bowling teams (where teamwork is minimal, with results being determined by the simple addition of individual scores) or baseball teams (where teamwork is somewhat sequential, with one person batting and then another, with one person catching and then throwing to another), but rather soccer, basketball, or football teams—where motion is continual, where interplay between players is everything, where unplanned scrambling is frequent, and thus where skilled on-field leadership is demanding and constant.

3. This new breed of leaders will be seen as one of the church's most critical resources.

In times of no change, in times within one known paradigm, management and tradition can sustain an organization. But in times of change, in times between sequential paradigms or among many coexisting paradigms, strong and innovative leadership is air, water, sight, intelligence. Oddly, the value placed on leadership in the new church must continue to rise at the same time we are experiencing a renewed emphasis on the ministry of the laity and the corresponding de-emphasis on "clergy." A new sense of calling, of honoring the pastorate, of respect will be necessary in the leadership culture of the new church.

4. New approaches to training will be needed to produce this new kind of leader.

Because seminaries train scholars, and because scholarship and leadership require very different kinds of people and gifts, traditional seminaries will either shrink to the size needed to provide scholars only, or they will die, or they will retool themselves to become the seedbed of leadership development. Scholars will increasingly see themselves as valued consultants to leaders—as will leaders.

Because change will be continuous, learning will also be continuous, not concentrated in a few years at the beginning of one's career. Study sabbaticals will become more common. Books and libraries and teachers all will be available on-line, so "virtual schools" will deliver their services without dependence on campuses. School will come to the students more often, and the reverse will happen less. Increasingly, training and internship and granting credentials will become local church-based. Seminaries may become more like consultant agencies to local churches— facilitating creative thinking through think tanks, troubleshooting and assisting with crisis management, and—even more useful—

anticipating tomorrow's problems in advance. In the new church, seminaries could once again find themselves exciting places to be.

5. Leadership will have to become less damaging personally.

I am not alone in feeling that the pastorate can be one of the cruelest places on earth. In *The 21st Century Pastor*, David Fisher says,

> Being a pastor today is more difficult than anytime in memory. . . . Greg Asimakoupoulos began a review of two books on the pastoral crisis in *Leadership* magazine with these words: "Warning: the list of endangered species is growing. To bald eagles, koalas, and spotted owls, add another: ordained pastors energized by what they do." He goes on to claim that the majority of American ministers are suffering from burnout. . . . A friend . . . surrendered his credentials because, in his words, "I can't take the pounding any more." Why is it that so many of us begin with such high hopes and dreams and end up tired and discouraged?
>
> Psychiatrist Louis McBurney reports that low self-esteem is the number-one problem pastors face. Why? We are in a high-demand, low-stroke profession in a culture that does not value our product or our work. We labor among people with unrealistic expectations, and deep inside we expect far more from ourselves and the church. It's no wonder McBurney's study identified depression as the second most identified pastoral problem.[3]

Archibald Hart adds this:

> Contrary to what many laypersons believe, depression is a major occupational hazard for ministers. For many ministers, surviving the ministry is a matter of surviving depression. Mostly the depression is not a positive experience. It robs the minister of power and effectiveness and destroys the joy of service.
>
> It is impossible for anyone who has never been a minister to understand the loneliness, despair, and emotional pain that a large number of ministers must bear. Not a few leave the ministry altogether because of the debilitation of depression.

Others exist in their pastorates in an unhappy, dissatisfied, and disillusioned state rather than leave their churches or change vocations.[4]

Surviving the amazing expectations, the delicate power issues, the free-floating rage, the stress, the demands, the motive erosion, and the disappointments that every pastor faces before noon on Monday—it's not easy for any of us. On the other side, lay leaders will do more to protect and care for their professional staff, and professional staff will do more to protect and care for themselves—including availing themselves of mentoring, support groups, study breaks and sabbaticals, and the like. While we need to say "ouch" at least a little more, a little louder, and a little sooner, we in ministry can't empower the causes of our distress simply by blaming externals and thus making ourselves victims. Rather, we have to help forge solutions by designing a leadership lifestyle that is not suicidal.

6. At the same time, we can't pretend that leadership is an easy career, free of suffering.

God's leaders have always faced criticism, threats, misunderstanding, and unfair treatment—when they weren't facing nails, whips, knives, and clubs. There is no way around it: Church leadership has always been less a career than a calling. We do ourselves a favor by remembering that fact. A friend, a discouraged pastor who later left the ministry to save his mental health, told me once, "On top of all of the difficulties, somewhere we baby boomers got the idea that life was supposed to be easy, and if it's hard, we must be doing something wrong." One would think that Paul's writings in 1 and 2 Corinthians (not to mention Jesus' example) would prevent this misconception, but few of us—especially boomers—are up for Mensa memberships.

If suffering and difficulty are intrinsic to spiritual leadership at all times, how much more so today, when our calling as leaders is to transform organizations. William Easum put it this way:

Many books have been written on the process of transforming an organization. Most of them make far too much of the logistics involved. The process is simple; the sacrifice is often great. Transformation takes focus, tenacity, and a willingness to be crucified! Transformation is successful when God's people understand the high stakes for which they are playing. The problem with too many of our church leaders is that they no longer see ministry as a life-and-death issue. Too many clergy are professionals; too many laity see the church as just another association or club.[5]

When ministry is just a professional career for the clergy and church is just another association or club, when huge arguments arise over petty trivialities and huge denial arises over major issues, the church hardly seems worth sacrificing for. The root of our challenge is to see the church as a life-and-death matter for individuals and for our world—as something truly worth the suffering invested to save it and lead it and love it. Bill Hybels's simple declaration in this regard helps to explain his endurance through stress, criticism, and the dark sides of success: "I love the church. I am convinced it is the hope of the world. I think I understand why Christ called it His bride. And I humbly thank God every day for letting me be part of it."[6]

That language of love leads us to a final characteristic of the new breed of leaders.

7. Leadership must once again become a matter of love and spirituality, a place for spiritual sages, not just organizational technicians.

Henri Nouwen knew this:

It is not enough for the priests and ministers of the future to be moral people, well trained, eager to help their fellow humans, and able to respond creatively to the burning issues of their time. All of that is very valuable and important, but it is not the heart of Christian leadership. The central question is, are the leaders of the future truly men and women of God, people with an ardent desire to dwell in God's presence, to listen to God's voice, to look at God's beauty, to touch God's incarnate Word and to taste fully God's infinite goodness?[7]

Is it an exaggeration to say that the church faces a leadership crisis? In *Rediscovering Church*, Bill Hybels says, "Much is hanging in the balance. It's my conviction that the crisis of mediocrity and stagnation in today's churches is fundamentally a crisis of leadership."[8] And nowhere is the difficulty of leader better illustrated than in the chapters written by Bill's wife, Lynne, in that same book. If we have a leadership crisis now, how much greater will the challenge become as we move closer to the other side?

Unless the new church takes this crisis to heart, there will be no new church to speak of. Conversely, the new church itself will be the creation of a new breed of innovative, Spirit-guided leadership. Create a new clergy, and a new church will follow. It's the new leaders who will guide us into the other side.

We talk about saving whales, saving owls, saving unborn babies, saving the earth. Leaders may be equally endangered—and more valuable than we imagine. Because they try not to complain too much, we may be dangerously unaware of their pain until it is too late.

CLOSER TO HOME...

When I wrote the first draft of this chapter, two members of my staff were considering leaving the ministry. I spent two years on the verge of doing so as well, and many of my best friends have left—good people, people the church needed. The reasons for this exodus are many, but the conclusion is clear: Something about ministry is always hard, but these days it seems very hard, almost too hard.

Many pastors and other leaders blame themselves for their inability to continue in ministry, and many laypeople are happy to agree with them. Many mistake symptoms for the disease itself. Just as a fever isn't the disease but rather a way of coping with infection, maybe many leadership failures are effects rather than causes. For example, is it possible that some pastoral affairs are not just about lust, but rather about escape from an intolerable situation? Is it possible that depression and burnout are symptoms of the profession rather than the professional who happens to come down with them? At what point do we conclude that the epidemic of aborted pastoral careers requires a critique, not of the "quitters," but rather of the situation? When the rats leave the ship, do we critique the rats and assail their character?

STRATEGY NINE

If you are a leader thinking of quitting, may I offer you one piece of advice in the form of a plea? Please don't use a permanent solution to a temporary problem. If you need to quit, if you cannot continue without psychological and spiritual damage, then do what you need to do. But if there are precautions you can take, emergency measures that might help—sabbaticals, counseling, longer vacations, pleas for help, or even ultimatums to your board, accompanied by a photocopy of this chapter— please take them. Please try to save yourself, because your people might not understand, and they might not try to save you until it's too late.

A friend called me not long ago. "You've been a real friend to me," he said. "I just thought I'd let you know that I'm resigning my pastorate tonight. I'm getting out of ministry."

"I care about you," I answered, "and I hate seeing you get eaten alive, so I understand. But it's not like there's a long line of people better than you waiting in the wings to take your place. This may be good for you, necessary for you, but I can't help but think it's bad for the kingdom of God."

What hope can I offer? Only this: I believe this transition zone is temporary. If you think the conflicting expectations are insane, and the juxtaposition of trivialities and profundities maddening, and the relevance of training to reality pathetic, and the clumsiness of church structures infuriating—you're right. You're not crazy to demand better. But remember that you're in the transition zone. You're being asked to build skyscrapers in a time of high tectonic activity. You're being asked to run the hundred-yard dash in a tornado. It is an insane task, especially so during these peculiar times. [9]

But what if just surviving these times is actually a sign of huge success, like surviving a plague during the Middle Ages? What if one of your greatest accomplishments in life would be to simply "preserve the gene pool" by staying alive and fertile, spiritually speaking, to help colonize the new world on the other side? What if you just keep breathing and just hold out for one more day, swimming like crazy in a riptide, avoiding drowning for one more minute? And what if eventually you find yourself, choking but safe, in the warm sand on the other side—a survivor?

"How do you know?" you might ask. "How can you be sure this transition zone is temporary? How do you know that if I don't give up, it will be worth it on the other side?" And of course, I don't know, but I do believe. That's why I'm still here.

By the way, for you who *have* left ministry, please rest up and heal up. Take your time. Learn all you can. Perhaps this time is a sabbatical, and in the new church you will have a critical role to play again. Don't hide from your disillusionment, anger, or doubt. If God is a God of truth, the way ahead must be the way through, acknowledging reality with eyes wide open. You will help us more by saying what you really think and feel; the church needs your honest data, no matter how painful. You probably couldn't have been this honest if you still were in the saddle.

Remember that there's no shame in being injured on the front lines.

Subsume Missions in Mission

*Understand the crisis in
world missions, and help launch
a new missionary movement.*

On the wall of my office hangs a picture of my grandfather when he was about my age. He was a missionary—a "real" missionary, in safari clothes, in Africa, standing with a gun next to a lion he killed. The lion had eaten some villagers a few nights before. My grandfather looks confident: saving lives, saving souls, all in a day's work. The lion looks dead.

My grandfather faced many hardships to be a missionary. After his first wife, my grandmother, died, he was left with seven children to raise. One of his sons almost died "in the bush," as they called the rural areas of Africa. My grandfather walked literally thousands of miles and faced real dangers during his service for the Lord.

It wasn't an easy life, but the results were real. People who had never heard the gospel were converted, churches were established, and parts of Angola today still bear the marks of his ministry.

Now missionary work is much easier: hours-long plane rides instead of months-long ship passages; ready access to medical care; government protection; E-mail for instant communication; credit cards for unexpected expenses!

And now missionary work is also much harder. I served for seven years as board chair for International Teams, a missions organization that has a reputation for integrity, quality, good missionary care, and innovation. Yet all the missionaries I have met agree on one point:

This thing is hard. In spite of all the advances and advantages, today's missionary challenges seem every bit as daunting as those my grandfather faced. Every time I go to headquarters, each time I read a missionary prayer letter or E-mail report, each time I have been privileged to visit the people on the field, I realize that just as the local church is reeling in crosscurrents of change, so is the whole missionary movement.

James F. Engel of Eastern College has seen the changes and offers this challenge: "Are we willing to respond in a creative and entrepreneurial way to this period of turmoil resulting from shifting paradigms?"[1]

A LONG LIST OF PROBLEMS

*W*hy is missions so hard? Why do we feel more like the lion in the old photo and less like my grandfather? Why does the modern missionary movement seem to be losing steam? Sitting in the plane as I returned from the most recent mission board meeting, I penciled twenty-one reasons.

1. It seems as if we're almost done.

When I was a boy and my grandfather and his comrades visited with their slide projectors and box of animal skins and blow guns and spears, it was clear that we had a long way to go. But now, with Christian radio and television blanketing the world, with the term "Iron Curtain" having become an archaism, and with reports of churches springing up nearly everywhere, the need seems lessened, the task closer to being finished. We have moved the ball from deep in our territory to the opponent's two-yard line—we think—and the last few inches don't inspire us as much.

2. Denominationalism is dying.

Many Christians do not mourn the waning of denominational loyalties and identification, but the fact is that denominationalism helped the missionary movement. Who cares that the Presbyterians had already entered Korea successfully, since we Baptists had not yet planted our flag there? So what if there were already five

STRATEGY TEN

evangelical churches in that town in Mexico (not to mention the Roman Catholics); the fact that there were none there of our brand meant that we had a missionary duty. That was thirty years ago. Now such thinking seems gauche. The dying of denominationalism thus seems to be knocking some of the wind out of our missionary sails.

3. Urbanization has stolen the jungle mystique.

I must admit, palm trees and teeming rivers have an appeal that smoggy barrios and Russian-made high-rises lack. As masses of people have moved into cities in the last hundred years, the missionary frontline has moved from jungle path to traffic jam. Some of the romance of missionary life got left behind with the palm trees. You don't shoot many rogue lions anymore (although you may be shot by a drug dealer, or you might get AIDS in the hospital—two forms of death that similarly lack anything close to romance or mystique).

4. The home church is struggling.

When the home base is struggling, it is more difficult to get excited about sending our brightest and best people, and our needed dollars, overseas. And the missionary's career may outlast our church anyway. And although it's hard to admit it, if we are so weak here at home, maybe we don't really have that much to offer people far away. If we lack credibility here in Jerusalem, why should they believe us in Judea, Samaria, or Timbuktu?

5. The home church is selfish.

Even if we are not struggling as a church, we may still be self-preoccupied. We need another concert, another seminar, another Christian television station—quickly! Who was it who said, "The greatest threat to world evangelism is the church preoccupied with her own existence"?

6. The world is becoming more educated.

Christians seem to have fared better in evangelizing the less educated than the more educated people of the world for the last several hundred years. As Europe became more intellectual, the missionary frontier moved to America; then as America grew more educated, the frontier moved to Africa, South America, and Asia. But where do we go as the countries on those continents steadily catch up with the rest of us?

7. Christianity seems to have failed.

To the Muslim world, every rerun of *Dallas* (isn't that in the Bible belt?) or *Baywatch* (isn't that in California, the land of megachurches?) offers living proof that Christianity hasn't succeeded very well in making Americans into better people. From the Civil War in America to the Rwandan genocide, from illegitimacy in American churchgoing teens to the spread of AIDS among young African Christians, from televangelists' scandals to rising divorce rates among fundamentalists, Christianity doesn't seem to stop Christians from killing and enslaving and hating and fornicating any less than people of other religions or no faith. If Christianity can't solve poverty, racism, or family breakdown, does it really deserve the sacrifice of missionary endeavor? Harsh words, perhaps, but I don't think I am the only one who has ever thought them.

8. Postmodernism and pluralism make this a different world.

It has been a long time since the missionary movement had a challenge like postmodernism staring it down. Jungles and lions are one thing; a profound and deep-seated worldwide skepticism about the capacity of human beings to know anything with certainty is another. Add to this a hunch that the most heinous crimes in history were perpetrated by people overly sure of themselves, people passionately committed to a cause, people who wanted to change the world—and you just may very quickly scare away the most thoughtful people from the whole missionary endeavor.

9. The spiritual–material polarization has been difficult to overcome.

We have all known that the best missionary impact occurs when proclamation and demonstration coincide, when the words of the gospel are illustrated by the deeds of the gospel, when compassionate action accompanies passionate communication. However, it has been harder than we thought to keep that balance. Where the church has focused on deeds, too often the message has seemed to lose its urgency; where we have focused on words, too often the deeds have been forgone; and where we have sincerely tried to keep the balance, we have tended toward one or the other extreme over time. The result? The ideal of a balanced endeavor has usually eluded us.

10. The proliferation of parachurch groups and workers has caused donor fatigue.

Market saturation has become a real factor in the missionary force. It is not that the secular world is saturated with spiritual resources (although religious radio and cable television can give us that impression sometimes), but that the Christian community has been besieged by too many appeals from people in ministry. Donors can't say yes to every appeal, so sooner or later, they must start—and will keep on—saying no.

Donors face another problem created by the growth and success of parachurch ministries. A new, young, revolutionary parachurch organization attracts entrepreneurial pioneers. Those visionary Peters and Pauls tend to create excitement (and often a little chaos as well) while attracting funds wherever they go, so an entourage of organizers and mess-cleaners is needed in their wake. The organizers and cleaner-uppers tend to be more sedate people, less inspiring and therefore harder to fund. Moreover, as the organization gains a following, it tends to become well run, complete with health and retirement benefits—and long lists of rules, policies, and procedures. These last almost guarantee that entrepreneurial pioneers—the very people who spurred the movement early on—will steer clear as more sedate, stable people get on board. The organization, now perhaps bloated organizationally, requires more and more funds to survive and delivers less and less of the excitement and zest that rewarded the early donors. Yesterday's success has become today's problem.

11. A lack of dramatic results can cause cynicism.

I once was seated next to a missionary pilot at a banquet. "An exciting job you have—getting to meet so many missionaries," I remarked, trying to stimulate some polite conversation. He grunted something.

I followed up: "What impressions do you have of missionaries these days?"

"They fix their cars a lot."

Too often, poor training, inadequate project design, ineffective leadership, weak missionary care, unfortunate selection and screening, and the ability to write prayer letters that exaggerate actual performance all combine to keep missionaries on the field who are long on sincerity and short on results. This lack of results discourages potential missionaries and donors alike, especially if they don't like fixing cars.

12. There are too many unsatisfied missionary customers.

They were young and idealistic. They were told, "Come with us for two years and change the world!" They heard, they raised support, and they went. And they tried—and the world didn't change. So they signed on for an additional two years, then four. Then, exhausted, they realized that the world wasn't really going to change, at least not as much as they had anticipated. They had fallen victim to an effective appeal that was neither realistic nor in their best interests. The ensuing disillusionment hurts them, and as the missionaries come back demoralized and jaded, it hurts all those who supported them.

13. There has been a reaction against the "ugly American" stereotype.

In this complex world, two seemingly opposite things can be simultaneously true. On the one hand, we have the "ugly American" missionary organization—with back-slapping, thumbs-up Yankees smiling big and praising the Lord like a TV evangelist, devising grand strategies and revolutionary intitiatives that make about as much sense as using the word "crusades" in Muslim countries. Here they come with mass mailings full of SINCERE CAP-

ITAL LETTERS and *urgent italics* (and maybe even underlinings in RED) to raise support for the latest project, which is guaranteed to "reach the world" by the year 2020 (a number that has a very nice sound to it, and a certain visionary ring).

Never mind that nobody has defined what in the world is meant by "reaching the world," or that there are already many indigenous Christians in the areas they target—Christians whom they have *never even consulted*, much less involved in their big plans. Never mind that these well-meaning missionaries thus show even less sensitivity to a foreign culture than they generally do to their own back home. No wonder so many folk around the world gag when they hear of another effervescent plan coming from us big-hearted but seemingly small-brained North Americans!

On the other hand, the reaction against the ugly American stereotype can be nearly as tragic: Think small, do nothing daring or prophetic or entrepreneurial, never offend the indigenous Christians (who may have become as ineffective at reaching their culture as many North Americans have become back home), don't innovate, don't act American even if that's what you are. Meanwhile, North American popular music, film, and culture in general are—for better or worse—arguably the most universal cultural phenomena in the world. So ironically, just as the missionary movement begins to feel snobbish toward all things American, more people around the world have more in common with North Americans than ever before, and that number will likely increase for the time being.

Our desires for cultural sensitivity are good, and I thoroughly affirm them, but we must not be reactionary. There is more than one way to get off the track. We need the kind of wisdom and savvy suggested by veteran missionary-theologian Lesslie Newbigin:

> The danger inherent in all programs for the "indigenization" or "acculturation" of the gospel is that they involve the church with the conservative and backward-looking elements in the society. A study of the missionary history of the nineteenth century will show, on the other hand, that some of the foreign elements that were accepted by the converts from the missionaries were welcomed precisely *because* they made a break

with the traditional culture and therefore came as reinforcement for younger elements in society who were impatient of old tradition. And where foreign missionaries, bearers of a culture considered (rightly or wrongly) to be "advanced," have tried to confine the "indigenous" church to the traditional language and culture of the past, they have been deeply and rightly resented. It is sufficient to mention the word "apartheid" to make the point.[2]

14. The indigenous missionary movement has grown at the expense of the traditional missionary movement.

In recent decades many Western Christians have discovered the wisdom and economy of supporting indigenous missionaries rather than sending their own. The logic is compelling. For example, you can barely support one Western missionary in Nepal for $48,000 per year, but that same amount can support twelve Indian missionaries. Those Indian missionaries will have fewer cultural adjustments, more facility with the language, and fewer political restrictions, so it almost seems sinful to waste money on Westerners.

Now, I hasten to state that I am in favor of indigenous missionaries. But we need to be realistic on two points. Jesus didn't say, "Give money, so someone else can go and preach the gospel in faraway lands." The Great Commission, which tells us to "go into all the world," doesn't let us off the hook that easily. Second, one of the ugliest things Americans and other Westerners can do is to corrupt their Third World brothers with unwise infusions of money. Stories are told of indigenous missionaries who were receiving considerable sums of money from as many as three Western organizations—each unaware of the donations of the others, and all unknown to the local Christian community that was also supporting them financially.[3]

I believe it is vitally important to encourage indigenous missionaries, but I don't believe Western missionary passion needs to grow weaker for the worldwide movement to grow stronger. I sometimes wonder if we aren't falling thoughtlessly into the trend of exporting jobs overseas to take advantage of cheap labor—a trend with definite short-term economies but long-term consequences that warrant more attention.

15. Mission agencies are unsure of their constituencies.

At first, mission agencies probably regard the spiritually lost as their primary constituency—that is, those whom they most want to communicate with and serve. Then they often gradually come to view their donors as their constituency. Eventually, their missionaries, both on the field and in retirement, may crowd out even the donors. This is an understandable phenomenon, but it is also an undesirable one if we care about evangelism.

16. Missionaries continue to struggle with enculturation.

The first wave of the modern missionary movement, led by the British churches, tended to bring English culture along with the gospel. Today we can go to the Central Asian republics and find Korean missionaries bringing Korean culture along with the gospel. Before long, cultural differences (for example, many Korean Christians pray loud and in unison; British Christians usually don't) will become the basis for sectarianism and division among Central Asian Christians (for example, praying loud is viewed as more spiritual—or more fanatical). This will in turn hinder the spread of the gospel, since its adherents will no longer love one another.

17. Diversification is a blessing and a curse.

A friend of mine was a missionary to people who live on sailboats. Another is a missionary to professional golfers. There are medical missionaries, musical missionaries, and missionaries devoted primarily to racial healing. There are missionaries who specialize in caring for other missionaries. Some missionaries dig wells in Christ's name, and others lend funds to start small businesses. I can imagine a missionary movement that does ecological cleanup in Christ's name. All these facets of Christian mission are compelling enough to attract some people to give their lives and others to give their money, and this we all applaud. But after a while, when the word "missions" seems to mean almost anything, we have to wonder if it means anything in particular. The loss of focus can result in many other losses, too—a loss of commitment, accountability, interest, funding, and purpose. If diversification is to continue, we need some grand unifying themes that make "mission" mean more than "anything one does requiring financial support and a passport."

18. Many missions face structural chaos.

Suppose a mission begins working in Africa. Eventually, it divides Africa into regions—perhaps North, Central, and South. Soon it begins work in Asia, and then South America. At this point, the mission may reorganize and deal with Africa as a single entity again. Or it may decentralize and deal on a country-by-country basis. Right about that time it starts a work among refugees, people leaving one country to live in another. Under which country should the refugee work be recognized: the originating or destination country? And what if the refugee missionaries in different places want to organize themselves separately from the other departments, since refugee work in Rwanda has much in common with refugee work in Thailand or Germany? Then add a youth division (which is also cross-national) and a radio division and a medical emergency team (which moves from place to place)— and pretty soon, you have organizational charts that require five dimensions for display.

But we're not done yet. If the missionary work in Mexico is successful, soon you have Mexican missionaries going to Morocco. How do you fit them into your organization? Do you set up a separate Mexican organization, and if so, how does it relate to the parent organization? And what do you do when a church planted in the Moroccan mission field sends missionaries to Chicago to reach immigrants living there? Home, foreign, sending, receiving—the terms start to mix like watercolors, but it's not a pretty picture organizationally.

Choosing between organizational bureaucracy and chaos is a tough choice. Neither promotes missionary effectiveness very well. Paul McKaughan sums it up this way:

What was once a very neat package of home missions and foreign missions has become all mixed up and will be increasingly so. Truly distinct categories of ministry based on geography will become increasingly difficult since geography as a descriptor for type of business or product is virtually irrelevant in the anytime/anyplace world we live in.[4]

19. The focus on short-term reportable results has caused long-term damage at home and abroad.

Urgency has been a hallmark of evangelistic fervor: People need the Lord, and they need him today, and since the world is going to hell in a handbasket, you'd better get the lead out and get going before it's too late! In addition, big round numbers and big goals have been very effective at attracting missionaries and funds: Let's reach 2,000,000 people by sending 20,000 missionaries to 200 countries by the year 2000.

Sadly, these big goals have sometimes appeared to work, and prayer letters have gone back home praising God for the fact, to the encouragement of the donors. But come back to the so-called miracle site a year later, and what do we find? New believers? New churches? Too often we find nothing. Actually, we may find less than that. We may find people who are now disillusioned and cynical because they responded to a presentation of the gospel but had no follow-up.[5] Back home, donors eventually catch on and become as jaded as the ersatz converts across the globe. The long-term costs for these short-term "results" are high indeed.

20. Nominal Christianity has turned up on nearly every mission field.

Euro-American-style nominal Christianity isn't just for Europeans or Americans anymore. Just as we can find "born-again Christians" cohabiting in Baltimore and using drugs in Short Hills and showing bigotry in Biloxi and enjoying shameless materialism in Orange County, we can also find appalling levels of nominalism in Kenya, the Philippines, and Peru. A friend of mine is a missionary on a small island in the South Pacific. This island was evangelized over a hundred years ago, and everyone knows hymns and Bible verses—they are taught in every school—but relatively few of the people really seem to be Christians in any way except in name.

Eddie Gibbs sees urbanization, secularization, and pluralism combining to create a global wave of nominalism in the years ahead. Until he drew attention to the problem, few even seemed to recognize that the world of the twenty-first century will be markedly different from any previous century—precisely because most of the world now has heard of Jesus, and much of the world professes a nominal faith in him.[6]

Some years ago, evangelicals shook their heads as the pope talked about the need to re-evangelize much of Roman Catholic Latin America. But the situation isn't very different in many places where evangelicals have held sway for a decade or two. Our first missionary movement specialized in evangelism; maybe the next will have to specialize in re-evangelism, which may be an even tougher task (consider France, Italy, or Greece).

21. Women and ethnic minorities are still largely excluded from mission leadership.

The exclusion of women and minorities from leadership hurts the church in many ways. First, it means we miss important contributions from nonwhite male Christians. Second, it means we are subject to the unchecked biases of white male Christians. Third, it means we present a huge stumbling block and lose credibility with contemporary, educated people for whom racism and sexism are deeply offensive signs of backwardness and injustice. Fourth, it means we miss an opportunity to illustrate and validate the gospel message by demonstrating unity in diversity in Christ. Fifth, it perpetuates the myth that Jesus was white and that Christianity is a white man's religion. Sixth, since women in particular have played a very important role in Christian missions, their exclusion from leadership guarantees that we aren't listening to some of our most seasoned missionaries.

A SHORT LIST OF SOLUTIONS

*F*ortunately for all of us, my plane landed at this point, interrupting my mania of problem identification. Otherwise, I may

STRATEGY TEN

have lengthened the list even more, depressing us all beyond any point of recovery!

More fortunately, there is a list of possible solutions, and this list is shorter. (A short list is good since it is less overwhelming.) As we move toward the other side and a new missionary movement takes shape, I think that movement will incorporate several kinds of solutions, the first of which is probably the most far-reaching.

1. Emphasize project design.

The word "project" has fallen on bad times in missions circles, precisely because "projects" are seen as short-term, ugly-American initiatives, attractive to donors, often designed for maximum visibility, but seldom planned with enough concern for side effects and long-term impact. Having thrown out the baby with the bath water, we would do well to go hunting for the baby again.

Projects on the other side will probably have the following characteristics:

a. The project should have clearly stated primary goals along with desired auxiliary outcomes. (See more on goals later.)

b. The project should define the job descriptions needed to fulfill the goals. Qualified personnel should be sought to fill these specific job descriptions. The various tasks should be integrated into balanced teams, with special attention paid to finding qualified, spiritually gifted leaders and administrators to empower and support the teams. (This order—project design, team design, then recruitment—is notably absent from standard missionary recruitment strategies today.)

c. The project should have milestone dates, when progress reports will be submitted and funding can be reevaluated. It should be commonplace to discontinue projects that aren't working out. (Projects that go full term without producing the desired results should be seen as failures; those that are discontinued sooner should be seen as experiments, "nice tries," learning experiences, and opportunities to "fail forward.")

d. The project should have a firm completion date. When the project is completed, the missionary can seek funding for a new project, whether in the same field or elsewhere. Thus there will be many career missionaries, but few if any career-long projects.

e. The project should capitalize on strategic alliances whenever possible, to avoid needless duplication of effort or omission of expertise. Success seems more likely if several organizations contribute their best expertise to a well-designed joint project.

f. The project should involve written contracts or agreements for purposes of clarity. These contracts would assure donors that their money is being invested in an environment of accountability.

g. Whenever possible, projects should become self-sustaining or obsolete. For example, suppose the project is to plant a church in a certain barrio; once a self-sustaining church has taken root, the project becomes obsolete. If the objective is to wipe out a disease-carrying mosquito from a certain region, the project becomes obsolete once the insect is gone. If the objective is to train two hundred national youth leaders so they can develop vibrant youth outreach in their cities, the project becomes obsolete as soon as the two hundredth youth worker is trained; if those workers are trained to train others, so much the better—the project has become self-sustaining.

h. Whenever possible, the total cost should be clearly estimated up front for the life of a project. This enables donors to evaluate the potential benefits against the cost. (If missionary activities over the past twenty years were audited this way, some embarrassing money pits would be revealed—along with some amazing bargains.)

i. Project planners should assume there will be some unintended negative effects, and they should try to anticipate and overcome these effects. For example, a project to fund indigenous missionaries could unwittingly provide opportunity for corrupt practices by people seeking to take advantage of the endeavor.

j. Projects should have a wide compass that embraces factors such as the involvement of sponsors; involvement of the indigenous church; recruitment, coaching, and the care and ongoing training of the workers.

I envision two incubators for these kinds of projects. First, experienced mission agencies could develop them. In fact, well-conceived projects could become the primary "product" of these agencies. The distinguishing feature of successful agencies of the

STRATEGY TEN

future may well be their track record in effective project design and management.

Second, visionary leaders could dream up projects, then "shop" for a mission agency to fund them.

This mention of funding brings us to the second solution in our short list.

2. Raise new money in new ways.

Many Christians lament the demise of the old fund-raising strategies. Missionary deputation just isn't what it used to be, for many of the reasons we have already cited. New money for the missionary movement on the other side will have to be raised in new ways.

I envision something like the following. The new mission agencies will design exciting new projects. They will recruit—from both the present and the potential missionary labor force—people suited to the jobs and teams required by the projects. With their portfolio of projects, the agencies will solicit support from wealthy individuals, churches, corporations, and rank-and-file potential donors. Individuals will also solicit funds, as in the past. Both kinds of solicitation would have these kinds of boundaries:

a. There will be a time limit. An agency might ask for $50 per month (or $50,000 per year, or whatever) for a maximum of five years, with clear kick-out points if the project is not measuring up to defined standards along the way.

b. There will be a defined outcome. Donors will have something tangible to point toward during their time of giving, and something to celebrate when the job is done. (One problem I failed to list on the airplane is that we too seldom get to celebrate. Nehemiah's wall was finished, and they celebrated; David's temple was completed, and they celebrated; Moses' tabernacle was finished, and they celebrated. But we seldom define our projects in a way that allows for celebration.)

c. Successful completion of one project will help prepare donors for even more enthusiastic giving for the next project.

d. The measurability and accountability of this approach will discipline mission agencies to be realistic yet daring in their goal setting, a balance that has been very hard to sustain in the old regime.

Of course, there are other new ways to raise money—by not raising money at all. Suppose a Christian opens a huge hotel in an Asian country. She will strategically place a few Christians in management, with all the staff being Asians with non-Christian backgrounds. Perhaps one of her goals will be to bring a positive Christian witness to every staff person and guest who enters the hotel. And perhaps she will have one section of one floor of the hotel designated as living quarters for the domestic workers, all of whom are recovering drug addicts whose recovery is being supported and encouraged from an in-house, Christ-centered, twelve-step approach. And perhaps a local restaurant owner, also a Christian, is influenced by her example and begins hiring ex-convicts, teaching them to read and sharing the gospel as he helps them readjust to life on the outside through gainful employment. And perhaps a Laundromat owner catches the vision and begins hiring local teenagers with the desire to show them Christ by treating his employees well. There are a thousand reasons why each of these ideas might not work, but that is fewer than the ten thousand reasons why our current approach won't work in tomorrow's world. So perhaps such ideas deserve more than a passing thought.

3. Think outside the box.

In a changing world, crazy things happen. For example, maybe missionary work, which by definition seems to be about sending, will be more about bringing. Or maybe there will be no more short- or long-term missionaries. Or maybe there will be mission agencies with no missionaries at all. Let me explain what I mean.

a. Think *bringing*, not just *sending*. Suppose we send out some talent scouts, say, to churches in Western Europe. With the help of local pastors, we find fifty sharp Christian teenagers who have demonstrated they are leaders. We develop a series of summer experiences for their high school years: One summer we send them to work among the poor in Asia; the next, we bring them to the States to serve as counselors in a foreign-language summer camp;

after that, we set up internships in some of the most vibrant churches in the world. Maybe by bringing these fifty young people into a world of new environments and experiences, we will do more to affect their countries and the church spiritually than by sending fifty American missionaries into their cultures—maybe.

b. Think *fewer,* not *more.* There are at least a few Christian churches in most of the countries of the world today. When we send missionaries to these places, we may be co-opting some work that the native Christians should be doing, thereby weakening their motivation. If we sent fewer missionaries, but the few we sent were catalysts whose sole aim was to motivate, recruit, equip, and deploy local Christians in ministry, very possibly the church could do more with less. Even where there are no churches, we may learn that sending one A-plus missionary will be more effective than sending ten B-plus missionaries.

c. Think *term,* not *short* or *long.* If missions activity becomes more project-based, then everyone will work on terms. There will be no career missionaries in the old sense; everyone will work on terms determined by a particular project.

d. Consider the missionary-less mission agency. As the world becomes increasingly boundary free, as English becomes a global language, as companies send employees around the world more and more routinely, and as the Internet connects everybody to everyone instantaneously, perhaps mission agencies will design projects that involve laypeople only. The only staff will be project designers, recruiters, fund-raisers, and logistical support. All the labor will be fulfilled by laypeople, church staff, or "tentmakers"— Christians who arrange their business life to allow maximum time for ministry. Thomas Wolf, chair of the missions department at Golden Gate Seminary, writes, "Tentmaking is the most significant personnel deployment trend in missions today. Its importance will become even more apparent in the next decade, unless the baby is suffocated by the umbilical cord of the old paradigm."[7]

4. Launch a revolution in stewardship.

Many people are forecasting financial doom and gloom around the next corner, or at least the corner after that. But maybe they're wrong. Maybe the next hundred years will lead to increasing prosperity for much of the world. If that should be the case, one of the most strategic initiatives for the missionary movement would be to launch a worldwide revolution in stewardship. Communism has proved to be the laughingstock of the twentieth century—a grand idea that failed. Capitalism could prove to be the laughingstock of the twenty-first if the profit motive isn't complemented by the impulse to generosity.

One can argue endlessly over tithing: Is it or is it not the biblical standard for today? All biblical arguments aside, it just doesn't make sense for Christians on an island of affluence to be greedy in a sea of great need. The missionary movement on the other side would be wise to elevate a new kind of hero: the giver. That would be the businessman who tempers his standard of living so he can raise his standard of loving and standard of giving. That would be the middle-class American Christian family that gives 20 percent of its income to God's service: 10 percent to the local church and 10 percent to special missions projects. What would happen in this world if Christians became known for loving generosity instead of exaggerated rhetoric or angry politicism?

5. Think younger and younger, and older and older.

As the Christian movement begins its third millennium, perhaps it is like a man reaching his thirties, who is beginning to think long-term. He starts thinking about buying a house and maybe getting life insurance and beginning some investments. He starts thinking about ten- and twenty-year goals instead of ten-minute and two-week goals. His maturity teaches him that in addition to being short, life is also long—long enough that some long-range planning makes sense.

Granted, Christian eschatology can throw a wrench into these gears (see Strategy 11), but leaving Armageddon aside for a moment or two, what would happen if a group of missionary strategists sat down and asked, "How can we make this a more God-honoring world one hundred years from now?" I suspect they would reach this conclusion: Concentrate on children. They would say, "Think about the kind of people we need in the world of the future, and begin with the children. Use schools, summer camps, after-school and summer activities, books and tapes and Internet sites, wilderness experiences, television and radio, music and movies and art to build new generations of Christian kids."

Since studies show that most practicing Christian adults made serious faith commitments between the ages of thirteen and eighteen, perhaps we need to put, say, 80 percent of our missionary emphasis on kids under the age of eighteen. Since it is very likely that most churches won't change, perhaps we need to try to create exciting youth churches within stagnant adult churches, so that when the youth get to be twenty or thirty, they can either take over their parents' (and grandparents') churches or, more likely, start their own. Since the majority of people in many parts of the world are under eighteen, perhaps that's where we should invest the most energy. And since most adults love kids, maybe the best way to get through to adults is by doing fantastic things for their kids—like showing them the love of God and exposing them to life's greatest experiences, including good, clean fun.

According to Paul McKaughan (writing abou the twentieth century),

> More babies will be born in the last quarter of the present century than in all of previous history. There are more kids in Mexico City under 15 than the entire population of Los Angeles. Bob Linthicum of World Vision in *Together* magazine April-May of '94 says there are more children in Calcutta than people in Chicago and 70% live in the slums and on the streets. He goes on to say that by 2000, 10% of the world's population will be poor children living in slums or in poor settlements of third-world cities.[8]

There are many reasons to say it: If you take the Christian mission seriously, think young and welcome the children to come to Christ.

Meanwhile, we also have to take into account that the number of senior citizens will surge worldwide. McKaughan predicts that by 2026, one-seventh of the world's population will be over the age of sixty. These seniors represent both an opportunity and a challenge for the Christian cause. They are a mission field, a source of missionary recruits, and a source of funds (through regular and estate giving) all in one. Through missions trips and "vision visits," as agency board members and consultants, these seasoned saints must be involved in the task of Christian mission.

Bob Buford argues in *Halftime* that more and more middle-aged people will decide to switch their attentions from success to significance.[9] Brad Smith of Leadership Network urges Christians to encourage the development of "social entrepreneurs"—successful, mature adults who can fund or staff important new ventures in their second half of life. These are all reasons to think older and older even as we think younger and younger.

6. Face the reality of the church.

As a pastor who has served with a mission agency, I see the church from both sides now. To the local church, mission agencies can seem like vendors who keep calling, calling, calling, wanting, wanting, wanting. To the mission agencies, local churches can seem like selfish, inefficient, tradition-bound, politics-paralyzed ghettos of wasted Christian potential.

The sad thing is, we can't avoid the church. Lead some people to Christ, bring them together, and like it or not, you have one. That is why of all people, mission agencies should be reading about the church and caring about the revitalization and liberation of the church on the other side.[10]

The exciting thing is that the church really is an amazing idea, especially when contrasted with the parachurch organization, which is also pretty amazing. Here's an offhand definition of both:

Church: A self-sustaining organization that does ministry and produces a surplus of energy and money over time. In other words, it attends to its own needs and, in so doing, miraculously generates more than it needs, so it can give to needs beyond its own borders.

Parachurch: An organization that does ministry, but in a situation (such as a prison, military base, college campus, or country without Christians) that renders it incapable of being self-sustaining. (The inmates have no income, or the soldiers or students get transferred or graduate, and so on.) The money and energy needed to sustain the parachurch generally come from the church.

Now here's the exciting thing: When we produce vibrant new churches, they become new profit centers—breaking the first law of thermodynamics, if you will—by creating energy and money where there was none before. Their surplus creates resources for parachurch ministries. But note the needed balance: If we have too many of the latter in relation to the former, we will have problems. That's why I foresee a resurgence of church planting (and reinvention) as a prime goal and missionary strategy on the other side.

BAD NEWS AND GOOD NEWS

So what is the bottom line?

The bad news is that missions as we have known it appears to be in decline and probably will become a casualty as we pass to the other side.

The good news is that mission—the mission of the church as salt and light in this world—faces exciting new prospects. In fact, in the new world, mission is all there is. At International Teams, the staff is fond of this quote: "The church exists by mission as fire by burning." This will increasingly become the slogan on the other side. After all, what good is the church if it has no salty or enlightening effect on the world around it? Shouldn't it then be trampled underfoot, as Jesus said (Matthew 5:13)? William Easum sums it up like this:

> . . . life in Christ comes to us on its way to someone else, congregations should focus outward instead of inward, congregations exist for those who are not part of them, life is meant to be given away not kept, God does not honor congregations that seek merely to raise money and survive.[11]

What does this mean? In a sense, missions will lose their special status, but the loss will be more than compensated as global mission becomes the heartbeat of the church. If we can subsume the old missions in a new, progressive, cooperative, comprehensive sense of mission, we have some thrilling days ahead indeed.

This change—from missions as a special (and optional) category of church life to mission as the primary focus of church life—will be far different from the old paradigm. But as Mike Regele says,

> . . . that paradigm is in shambles. We must be the church for others. If we embrace the notion that the local congregation is the front line of mission in the twenty-first century, then we must see mission as all that we do. We must begin to frame our understanding of mission as both near and far, as both time and money, and as both prayer and personal involvement.[12]

Every church a mission organization. Every Christian a missionary. Every mission agency a facilitator of the work of the church. Every neighborhood a mission field. We can hope that Christianity will be as inconceivable apart from mission as fire from burning. This will be one of the greatest legacies of the missionary movement—that it helped create this mission orientation in the church on the other side.

REASON FOR EXHILARATION

*I*n spite of my long, depressing list of challenges, I feel exhilarated because in recent years, through my association with International Teams, I have been able to watch a new generation of mission leaders team up to tackle these challenges and think in new ways. I know that other mission organizations are similarly doing some fresh thinking. But I do have one lingering fear: I worry sometimes that there are so many of us philosophizing about our mission, discussing it, reading and reading about it, holding conferences on it, critiquing it, and managing and administering it . . . that there are too few people to actually get out and do it!

I once read about a fishing association. Its members avidly studied fish, discussed fishing techniques, read books and magazines on angling, bought the best equipment, held meetings to indulge their fascination with fish lore, and in general led active, fish-oriented lives. But after a while somebody asked, "Has anyone actually caught one lately?" The room was silent.

STRATEGY TEN

I wonder at those words of Jesus regarding a plentiful harvest and the dearth of harvesters (Matthew 9:37). I am proud of my grandfather, who stood there with rifle in hand in the photo on my wall. I think he would be proud of us for doing the work we have been given in our generation, even though on the surface it would appear to be very different work from his. True, we don't need to shoot rogue lions much anymore, and many of his methods for ministry in the African bush wouldn't work in today's postmodern, urban world. But he actually got out there and did it. And there is no substitute for his method: facing dangers, taking risks, paying a price, loving neighbors, and trusting the Lord.

But I also have a feeling he would wonder about all this talk after a while. Right about now, he would be ready to put this chapter aside, get on his knees, and then hit the streets to find somebody to encourage, somebody to help, somebody to pray for, somebody to love with the love of Christ.

Look Ahead, Farther Ahead

*Anchor your hope in
the future rather than
the past, and explore a new
eschatology.*

*H*ere is a fundamental rule of the road: The faster you drive, the farther ahead you must look. Why? Because you will be there sooner at high speeds. Seeing a huge pothole or a stalled car 300 feet ahead isn't a problem when you're sputtering along at 25 miles per hour; you have plenty of reaction time. But the situation is different if you're tooling at 80; you really need to know about those obstacles 1,200 feet out there. As we cross over to the world on the other side—a world where we will all drive fast—we will need to look farther ahead in the road than ever before. We will still need every bit of our short-distance awareness—for that child darting out to chase a runaway ball or a puppy, for that black ice that formed overnight. But more than ever, we will need the ability to think ahead—and to think further ahead than we are used to doing.

REASONS FOR A FORWARD FOCUS

*I*nstead of thinking ahead one year, or five, on the other side we will talk about one hundred years ahead, and maybe more. Perhaps at the dawn of the third millennium of Christianity, we will give serious consideration to planning for the fourth. That kind of statement might seem ludicrous, even heretical, but I believe we need this long-distance vision for at least three reasons.

1. Effectiveness

Effectiveness in a fast-changing world requires new ways of thinking and planning. Traditional linear planning (first this, then that—the kind we're comfortable with) is becoming increasingly insufficient. A corporate analogy might serve:

Imagine the church as a watch-making company. A few decades ago, we could develop a five-year plan, introducing a new watch through a process of market research, design, testing, refinement, production, marketing, sales, and service. Then, anticipating its obsolescence due to competition and new technology, we would need to plan the next new model, perhaps with a new kind of band or new face design. So begins another five-year process.

That linear planning strategy, which may have worked in the old industrial world of watches and refrigerators, seems like a joke in today's world of hardware and software. Now, even before one product is through the design phase, five more generations are in process as well. The old idea of sequential short-term planning has been telescoped into a concept of overlapping, simultaneous plans, which, because they are elastic, actually serve to extend our thinking much further into the future. For the church to keep thinking and planning like old watchmakers helps guarantee ineffectiveness in a fast-changing world.

In fact, today's planning in innovative organizations doesn't concern itself only with the next models of the same old products. Innovative companies are anticipating the time when their whole product line will be obsolescent and some completely new technology will be needed. That involves looking beyond the horizon, not just at the 300 feet of road in front of you. If the church confines itself to old-fashioned, short-range, linear planning, it will be producing LPs and eight-track music tapes at a time when audiocassettes are already close to obsolescence, when innovators are anticipating downloading music from the Internet to programmable disks. So simply for the sake of our own effectiveness, we need to think longer term, to look farther ahead in the road, to be anticipators and not just reactors.

2. Love

Loving our neighbors also requires us to think longer term. We are like emergency-room technicians who have been assigned to care for a colony of AIDS patients. We know about triage, and we know about trauma, and we think we are comfortable with life-and-death situations. But what if a life-and-death situation is no longer counted in minutes or hours, but years? If we really care, we have to expand our services from triage to chronic-disease care and—if we are really wise and ambitious—to conduct research and try to find a cure for this thing.

True, our world has triage problems aplenty. But it is also increasingly aware that stitching its flesh wounds is no substitute for addressing the debilitating diseases that require long-term solutions. If we restrict ourselves to triage, we have little to offer as citizens or neighbors—not to mention as Christians—in facing these major, chronic, global issues. We are heavenly minded, perhaps, but we will be of little earthly good unless we learn to stretch our span of planning and concern.

For starters, we don't even see some problems as problems if we lack a long-term, global frame of reference. For example, ask many Christians today what the biggest problems facing our world are, and you will probably hear triage issues such as abortion, the breakdown of families, and homosexuality. Ask people with a long-term focus, and you will hear a completely different set of issues: overpopulation, increasing nationalism and ethnic tribalism (including religious fundamentalism), systemic poverty, urbanization, and ecology.

Again, many of us don't see these as problems because they may take one hundred or two hundred years to become critical. We aren't used to concerning ourselves with such distant dangers. But some of these problems are such that if they aren't anticipated and averted in their early stages, horrific forces are set in motion that may be impossible to control.

So if we fail to participate meaningfully in our world's struggle with its global challenges, we are showing little love for our neighbors, not to mention our own unborn great-great-grandchildren.

Such short-sightedness may be excusable in nonbelievers, but wouldn't biblical wisdom and love call us to greater caring?

3. The Incarnation

Most important, our theology of the Incarnation inspires and calls us to longer-term thinking. Perhaps some feel called to be quaint for Christ. Other Christians, however, feel that Jesus' incarnation (an event in the past that is always contemporary and always has a claim on us as Christians) sets an example of showing up on time, of being in touch with one's world in the present—not of it, but truly in it.

If this is true, living in the early church required Mediterranean Christians to be concerned with the relation of Jews to Gentiles in Christ. Living at the time of Columbus required European Christians to be concerned about the new world. Living in Germany in the 1930s required German Christians to be concerned about the rise of Hitler. And if all that is true, then surely living at this time in history requires us to think globally and longer term. In our lifetime we can literally rise in an airplane and see a whole city in one view; we can rise even higher in a spacecraft and see a whole country—no, a whole continent—no, the whole globe. Just being able to see a photograph of our blue-and-white globe suspended in space makes us different from every other generation in history. We see ourselves, our world, and our future differently as a result.

Dozens of other factors reinforce this global mindset. We have learned that we are all interconnected ecologically—that aerosol spray cans in Kansas can help rift the ozone layer in Antarctica and cause cancers in children in Argentina. We are learning how we are interconnected economically—that if Chinese families increase their standard of living so as to consume just ten more pounds of pork per year, the whole world will feel the impact in grain prices. We are learning how we are interconnected politically, so that ideas of freedom and democracy, spread by fax, phone, and online services can't be contained by Iron Curtains or concrete walls. To live in our world today means to think globally, and thinking globally requires addressing bigger problems that involve bigger time frames. This, then, is the way we as Christians must learn to think, simply because of the Incarnation.

Why? Because the Incarnation is about God's solidarity with our world. It is about God leaving his distance, his transcendence, his safety, his glory, and getting caught up with the muck and blood and tears and spit and history of our world. It says that caring means entering and feeling solidarity with the problems of our world, so that "their" problems are our problems, too. Otherwise, we are saying that we Christians, with our parachutes, can't be bothered with the other passengers on this plane that's going down and is about to crash.

So we must accept the challenge to begin thinking longer term, to look farther ahead down the road, to stretch our span of concern and planning. We have to do it for the sake of our effectiveness, out of love for our neighbors, and out of faithfulness to Christ, whose solidarity with this sinful world brought its salvation.

WHY IS IT SO HARD?

*T*his is a real struggle for us as we cross to the other side. We aren't used to looking far ahead at all. We're used to looking back. And it's not surprising why.

Everything in our theology seems to be about the past. I remember that as a boy in Sunday school, I wished I could have been born when God was alive on earth. History was really exciting when real miracles were really happening—big ones, not the flimsy little ones for today—the truly good old days of Bible times, when Red Seas parted and manna fell, when walls crumbled and the sun stood still. Or in the days of Jesus, or of the early church. But everything since then seemed to me to be such a disappointment. Every time we compared our tawdry, sinking world of today with the glorious, inspiring world of the Bible days, it left me with the sense that history was pretty much done; the interesting part was way back there in the rearview mirror, not out the side windows of today, and certainly not ahead in the road somewhere.

Older now, I realize that even in Bible times dramatic miracles were relatively few and far between—like grand slams that may seem common in the condensed story of a whole baseball season, but are pretty rare game to game. I realize now that even those miracles back then could have had many natural explanations, so perhaps they didn't seem any more incontrovertible at the time as many "acts of God" today. Now I am quicker to see the hand of God in daily events, especially in the "nonmiraculous miracles" of daily life and love and health and joy. But even now I see in myself, and in many other Christians, a residue of that Sunday school sensation that the best days are indeed behind us, that the decisive acts of history have already occurred, and that now we are basically living in the P.S. of a letter already complete, in the bottom of the ninth inning of a ball game decided by multiple grand slams back in the fifth.

This sense of history—that the weighty, significant part of history is behind us, that only the light ("lite"?) parts remain, insignificant by comparison with the old—is open for reexamination as we cross to the other side. The milestone of Christianity's second millennium invites reexamination and gets us thinking about an uncomfortable subject: eschatology.

REVISITING ESCHATOLOGY

Eschatology, the study of the last days and the end of all things, has in recent decades contributed to the problem we are considering here. Eschatology has too often discouraged us from looking ahead in a constructive way. There are two reasons why.

First, many evangelicals have held to a premillennial eschatology of immanence, urgency, and cataclysm. At any moment the Antichrist could appear and begin a period of tribulation and suffering, leading to the Battle of Armageddon and the end of history, followed by the final judgment and heaven and hell. Important? No doubt. Exciting? In a certain, perhaps morbid way. Attractive? As with going to the dentist for a root canal, you will feel better when it's over, but it's nothing to look forward to in the meantime. (Even if you believe you will be exempted by the rapture of the church, you still have to have some human sympathy for your friends, relatives, and neighbors who will have to endure this great tribulation.)

STRATEGY ELEVEN

Looking far ahead when we anticipate that the end is imminent seems useless if not faithless. The familiar analogy is worth repeating: Worrying about the long-term future of planet earth would be like rearranging deck chairs on the Titanic. The whole thing is doomed anyway, and the iceberg is closer than we think, so why bother? Better to warn the other passengers to prepare for disaster and man the lifeboats; better to focus on the afterlife and eternity since the time is so short. Ironically, this view of the future makes future history weightless, and keeps us living as people anchored to the past—when things seemed better.

Second, other Christians have followed a postmillennial option, whereby the church would exert greater and greater influence until the return of Christ would blossom like a rose from a bud (rather than rise from the ashes of destruction). The more liberal version of this postmillennialism, popular at the beginning of the century, was largely discredited by two world wars, a cold war, and a host of other scary problems that made it hard to say, without doubting or smirking, "Every day, in every way, it's getting better and better."

The conservative version, revived late in the century by some elements of the religious right, has given hope to a few, but has seemed to others like a kind of tribulation of its own. And even the hope it gave seemed linked to a short-lived shift in the prevailing political wind. Both versions of postmillennialism, it turns out, have this in common: They were more a reflection of American political hopes than universal spiritual hopes and therefore proved limited in their ability to inspire a motivating, weighty vision of the future.

Back in 1999, a series of novels in the category of apocalyptic fiction— no doubt riding the big wave of Y2K marketing fervor— rose to the top of both religious and nonreligious bestseller lists. The books gave one of the most popular of these twentieth-century American-style eschatologies a late great resurgence. It would be nice, in my opinion, if we could leave all of them in the last century and, in their place, develop a new vision of the future, one more along these lines....

1. An Eschatology of Hope

Jesus went everywhere preaching, "The kingdom of God is at hand." Loosely paraphrased, he was saying, "The kingdom of God is ahead in the road." It isn't behind us, back in "Bible times," as I thought in Sunday school. It is ahead of us. It is not here fully yet, though it is in some way among us; it is like a seed that has been planted and is growing; it is like yeast that has been added and is working; it is like a sun that is rising, with the day just ahead.

Few things could change the church on the other side as much as putting the weight on the future rather than the past. This means assuming that the best days are ahead of us, not behind; acknowledging that in this world we will have no shortage of tribulation, but will rejoice that God has an unspeakably wonderful future awaiting us. If we see the past as idyllic and wonderful (as we tend to do by idealizing Bible times, or the Reformation, or the Great Awakening, or the 1950s), and if we see the future as bleak and horrific (as we are prone to do after reading some contemporary apocalyptic fiction, or attending some old-fashioned dispensational "prophecy conferences"), no wonder we keep falling behind the times! No wonder we are looking back in our rear-view mirrors instead of ahead through our windshields! No wonder we are more often timid, depressed, or nostalgic laggards than bold leaders! What if we really believed that the best days are yet to be, that the kingdom really is just ahead in the road, beyond some rough spots, no doubt, but ahead nonetheless?

Consider how that simple but profound change in thinking could revolutionize us for the other side. Instead of casting ourselves as counterrevolutionaries, yearning for the good old days, scolding everyone for departing from the old paths, and asking the world to do the impossible—go back—we would cast ourselves as true revolutionaries, ahead of our time, living now by the love and reverence everyone will someday live by, calling everyone to get with it and be part of the new thing God is doing.

Leaning forward in this way, we will be filled with hope, not dread; energy, not nostalgia. We will look back on two thousand years of a slow, steady progress of the gospel, and we will say to the world, "You ain't seen nothin' yet." We will assume that God is still

STRATEGY ELEVEN

building and working—and will not become tired or distracted from his plans. True, tribulation is promised, but it is always dwarfed by the glory to be revealed. Hope indeed!

2. An Eschatology of Mystery

We would be making a huge mistake, however, to try to turn this hope into a concrete plan or scheme, as many pre- and postmillennialists alike have tended to do. Twenty centuries of church history should teach this, if they teach us anything: Anyone who claims to have the future figured out will turn out to be wrong. Jesus told us this at the beginning, but unfortunately that hasn't been enough to stop our speculations.

In the new church, if we are wise, we will finally get the point: Just as Jesus came the first time as a surprise—as prophesied yet surprisingly—so the end will come as planned by God, but not as expected by any of us. The end will combine justice and mercy, fear and hope, just as Jesus himself did, with many of the first coming in last, and many of the last, first. This sense of mystery may offend our rationalistic minds that demand, if not signs, thorough explanations. But the mystery itself is part of the message. We can assume if God wanted it clearer, he would have made it clearer. The world on the other side will have a greater respect for mystery, it appears, and so a weighty, hopeful mystery will be more acceptable to it—and, I believe, more faithful to the Bible.

3. An Eschatology of Urgent Patience, or Patient Urgency

The old eschatology, high on urgency and low on patience, argued for rapid and well-intentioned (if not always well-conceived) missionary work, always heavy with deadlines (by 1982! by 2000!). The new eschatology will aim to balance urgency and patience. Since a day with the Lord is like a thousand years, and since the opposite is also true, we have reason to believe that the end may not come for thousands of years, or even thousands of millennia (though it also may occur before you finish this sentence). Carl George addressed this balance between urgency and patience in his book *Prepare Your Church for the Future*:

I grew up with a keen awareness of living in the end times, in which Christ could return at any moment. This perspective motivated me to be ready and to pour my energies into things that will count for eternity.

Unfortunately, I allowed my "terminal generation" panic and zeal to keep me from visualizing an even bigger picture. . . . Today I'm still ready—and eager—for Christ's second coming. But I'm also asking, What if God delays two hundred years? What if, when we hit the year 2000, we're only at the halfway point of the church age, with two thousand more years to come? What kind of responses should I have made?

Suppose God has planned an extended future for the church? If so, our ministry dreams should receive the kind of planning appropriate to building a European cathedral rather than the all-too-common approach of throwing on another tar-paper patch that may last a whopping two or three years! When I meet the Lord, I don't want Him to ask, "Carl George, why did you check out so early?"[1]

If those long time frames seem repulsive, consider this: Paul and Peter would probably have found it equally repulsive to be told that Christ wouldn't have returned by now, don't you think? Could our world be in the same situation as Nineveh in Jonah's story—warned of destruction, yet mercifully spared—or of the captive Jews in Jeremiah's day—told to plant crops and seek the welfare of their host country? Could it be God's plan for all people through all time to live with this dynamic tension—not enough patience to breed complacency, and not enough urgency to inspire panic. Does he want us to hold urgency and patience in synergy to encourage us to plant trees (a long-term investment requiring patience) and plant them today (with enthusiastic urgency)? And could it be that on a personal level, urgency always makes sense, since each of us will face our own apocalypse (called death) within this generation anyway? And could it be that on a global level, patience also always makes sense, since God's plans and time frames make our longest life span seem like a sigh?

4. An Eschatology of Affirmation

The old eschatology of urgency without patience too often tended to devalue everything. If something's about to burn, why is it important? By contrast, the new eschatology must instill value rather than drain things of it. Jesus expressed this in the parable of the sheep and goats (Matthew 25:31–46), where no good deed is forgotten, where every little act of kindness done for the homeless, the criminals, or the hungry is instilled with eschatological importance. Rather than draining time of its value by submerging it into eternity, the new eschatology will infuse time with value through its connection to eternity.

5. An Eschatology of Ultimatum

If we dignify every act of love and kindness with eschatological significance, we must do the same with every act of selfishness or cruelty. So in the new church, without hysteria, without malice, without neurosis, we will live with the reality that all our actions count and that reality presents us, one and all, with an ultimatum: Because the kingdom of God is just ahead in the road, we must choose to repent now and live as part of the kingdom, or face the consequences.

Again, recognizing that we each have an appointment with our personal apocalypse within our generation, we can maintain a biblical sense of urgency and proclaim the reality of judgment. But we can do so with the dignity, confidence, "cool," and the class of Jesus, not with the angry, pathetic tone of parents who have lost control of their toddlers.

Our impatience on this side, Philip Yancey suggests, has been neither Christlike nor healthful:

> We sometimes use the term "savior complex" to describe an unhealthy syndrome of obsession over curing others' problems. The true Savior, however, seemed remarkably free of such a complex. He had no compulsion to convert the entire world in his lifetime or to cure people who were not ready to be cured. In Milton's words, Jesus "held it more humane, more heavenly first / By winning words to conquer willing hearts, / And make persuasion do the work of fear."[2]

On the other side, with a more balanced eschatology, we will be freer of the savior complex, less frantic and hysterical, and thus more like the Savior.

Such an eschatology, it seems to me, can be perennial, not annual like our current eschatologies, each tied to its present world situation and therefore each liable to extinction as the world changes. Such an eschatology will also help create a church that leans forward with a smile on its face and a gleam in its eye, not one that leans back with arms crossed, a sweaty brow, and nervous twitches. Those who hold this new eschatology, it seems to me, will be more likely to do more good in the new world—a world that will need people who are known by their good fruit, good attitude, good faith, and good hope.

MAKE IT SO

I must confess to being a *Star Trek* fan. I enjoy the new shows and reruns alike, and I enjoy pondering the vision of the future unfolded in the series. But as all fans know, in the *Star Trek* vision of the future, Christianity is almost invisible, as passé as telephone poles and wires. Spirituality is alive and well in various forms, and some Christian values seem to penetrate the Federation, but I don't recall ever hearing a single character identify himself or herself as a Christian.

This may simply be a reflection of the bias of the series' creator, Gene Roddenberry. But it might also suggest that the Christianity known on this side doesn't seem to fit with any imaginable future. I believe the Jehovah's Witnesses and the Seventh-day Adventists have something to teach us here. By identifying their eschatology with one century, whether nineteenth or twentieth, they effectively discredited their whole movements to some extent. Maybe we can learn that the only true eschatology must be timeless. To be honest, I get a feeling for both kinds of eschatology when I read the New Testament: a time-bound version, and a timeless version. But I think as we cross this particular historic threshold, more of the latter is what we need.

STRATEGY ELEVEN

Imagine a *Star Trek* episode in which the dramatic tension relates to turning the other cheek or refusing to judge others before judging oneself, complete with reference to Jesus' teachings. Or one in which, in the hopeless situation that generally comes just before the third commercial break, the captain brings the bridge crew into the ready room for a prayer. Or one in which the galley is filled each Sunday morning with people singing praises to the Creator as they look out the windows at a far quadrant of the galaxy.

Don't you think it is time to embrace an eschatology that will teach us to look hopefully ahead and farther down the road, that will turn the road into a runway and launch us through the clouds and maybe even to the stars? If Jesus were here today, would he be saying, "The kingdom of God is behind you" or "The kingdom of God is just ahead in the road"? We need a vision of the future, formed by our faith in the Lord.

Enter the Postmodern World—Part A: Understand It

*Understand postmodernism, and
learn to see it from the inside.*

Postmodernism is a rather bizarre term at first glance, a kind of absurdity rather like "pre-ancientism." However, its very oddness seems to be a good reason to keep it for now, because the concepts of postmodernism do seem odd, at least from an outsider's perspective.

To an outsider—that is, someone raised in another culture—the postmodern world is easy to critique, even to ridicule. But from the inside, it's not odd at all: It's just the way things are. (Think of a fish: Of all creatures, he knows the least about water, since it is all he knows and to him it isn't water—it's reality. The air, by contrast, is a hostile, alien, threatening place. Similarly, whether traditionalists, modernists, or postmoderns, we can hardly see our own position and nearly always see other positions as odd, inferior, inhospitable, and likely wrong.)

As Christians who want to live and love on the other side, we had better get a feel for postmodernity from the inside, because in many ways postmodernity is the other side, and it defines reality for more and more people.

WHAT IS IT?

*T*he term *postmodern* has gained enough attention that most people, although they don't know what it is, recognize it and feel guilty or embarrassed for not knowing what it is. (Some people are already tired of hearing it.) So what is it?

Bob Fryling sets up a useful contrast to contextualize the term in relation to traditionalism and modernism. He describes three people, each representative of a different cultural paradigm.[1]

1. The robed priest represents traditional culture, bound together by the priesthood's divine authority, revealed beliefs, sanctioned customs, absolute rules, accepted rituals, and meaningful holidays. The priest stands serene and content, if not a little offended by or afraid of the following two people and all they represent.

2. The scientist clad in white lab coat represents modern culture, feeling skeptical of and superior to traditional culture with its rules and superstitions. He (or she) stands erect and proud, boldly confident in individualism (I am free to pursue my own happiness), rationalism (research and reason can find the truth), technology (we can control and exploit nature to our own advantage), and progress (every day and in every way we're getting better and better).

3. The rock musician, clad in almost anything, represents the postmodern culture. He, she, or h/she is disappointed with, disillusioned with, and suspicious of both priest and scientist. He, she, or h/she doesn't stand, but rather slouches, gyrates, or dances with uneasy energy.

Beyond Fryling's illustration, we could consult Jacques Derrida, Stanley Fish or Michael Polanyi for a philosophical introduction to postmodernism. Or we could consult the Christian writers who have begun to address the topic. However, the former would require that we learn a sophisticated technical vocabulary—a little too far removed from everyday life for our purposes here. And unfortunately, too many (though not all) of the latter have been too quick to dismiss and oppose postmodernism before sufficiently understanding it.[2] But understand it we must if we are going to live effectively and love compassionately in the world on the other side.

So let us take a different route for exploration. One of the most popular movies during the nineties was *Jurassic Park*, based on Michael Crichton's dino-drama of the same name. Then came the sequel, *The Lost World*. True, the movie was little more than

STRATEGY TWELVE A

an extended chase scene, and neither book will be accused of being great literature. But like the best examples of popular culture, Crichton's books incarnate the spirit of the day. And instead of offering a view from the outside, they serve to put readers into the postmodern world so we can see the rest of the world, including the modern world, from its perspective.

Jurassic Park is the modern world. It is a dream of control. It is technology for fun and profit. But it is a dream gone awry. Nature, it turns out, has a stream of chaos running through it. And the modern story, it turns out, shows that the would-be circus masters are really just part of the circus—not so big or strong or wise after all. Both books end with the heroes in retreat, feeling lucky to have survived. And so it is for postmoderns looking at the modern world, which unleashed velociraptors of environmental degradation, T. rexes of ethnic oppression, and compies of lust and greed—we're lucky to have escaped alive.

But what can follow the decay of the modern dream? That question takes us to the last few paragraphs from *The Lost World*. A boatful of survivors speeds away from an island off the coast of Costa Rica. Ian Malcolm, a middle-aged scientist, has just offered a rather standard late-modern-world critique of man—cynical, disillusioned, bitter. Kelly, a junior-high-aged girl, responds to its bleakness by moving up to sit next to Doc Thorne, a more affable fellow:

> "Are you listening to all that?" Thorne said. "I wouldn't take any of it too seriously. It's just theories. Human beings can't help making them, but the fact is that theories are just fantasies. And they change. When America was a new country, people believed in something called phlogiston. You know what that is? No? Well, it doesn't matter, because it wasn't real anyway. They also believed that the four humours controlled behavior. And they believed that earth was only a few thousand years old. Now we believe the earth is four billion years old, and we believe in photons and electrons, and we think human behavior is controlled by things like ego and self-esteem. We think those beliefs are more scientific and better."[3]

To this point, Thorne sounds like any good inhabitant of the modern world, believing in science and progress. But he's not. Watch as the dialogue continues:

> "Aren't they?"
>
> Thorne shrugged. "They're still just fantasies. They're not real. Have you ever seen a self-esteem? Can you bring me one on a plate? How about a photon? Can you bring me one of those?"
>
> Kelly shook her head. "No, but . . ."
>
> "And you never will, because those things don't exist. No matter how seriously people take them," Thorne said. "A hundred years from now, people will look back at us and laugh. They'll say, 'You know what people used to believe? They believed in photons and electrons. Can you imagine anything so silly?' They'll have a good laugh, because by then there will be newer and better fantasies."
>
> Thorne shook his head. "And meanwhile, you feel the way the boat moves? That's the sea. That's real. You smell the salt in the air? You feel the sunlight on your skin? That's all real. You see all of us together? That's real. Life is wonderful. It's a gift to be alive, to see the sun and breathe the air. And there isn't really anything else. Now look at that compass, and tell me where south is. I want to go to Puerto Cortes. It's time for us all to go home."[4]

FIVE CORE VALUES

*T*his passage pithily illustrates five core values of postmodernism.

1. Postmodernism is skeptical of certainty.

As Thorne says, what we commonly call knowledge is really "just theories," and theories are just fantasies. In postmodernism, the analytical and critical rationality of modernism is taken one step further: It critiques not only the objective world and other people, but also the self and the self's very ability to know and understand.

STRATEGY TWELVE A

2. Postmodernism is sensitive to context.

Something can seem unquestionably true to people in a certain time period (such as Thorne's example of phlogiston for early Americans) or in a certain social group (consider the differences of opinion along racial lines regarding the trial of O. J. Simpson). But those same beliefs can seem silly and laughable to people in other contexts.

"Postmodernism gives value to many different contexts," explains Rinus Baljcu. "With its assumption 'every point of view is a view from a point,' it creates myriads of contexts. Every group of people forces you to find a common 'point.'"[5]

In other words, knowing is not an individual matter but a group experience. The groups we were born into or join will have a strong influence on what we know, or what we think we know.

3. Postmodernism leans toward the humorous.

We shouldn't take ourselves or anybody else too seriously. After all, if our perspectives are biased by the groups we belong to, if our understanding is limited by our contexts, if our view is valid only from our subjective standpoint, then each of us is untrustworthy and subjective in knowledge and judgment and none of us can presume to very much authority. In postmodernism, I am not going to be quickly intimidated by you and your claims to know the truth, nor am I going to expect you to be intimidated by me. And both of us had better be suspicious of any who try to force us to believe something just because they say so. After all, the worst atrocities in history (such as the Holocaust in Europe or the Pol Pot regime in Cambodia) were perpetrated by people who were absolutely sure of themselves.

Postmoderns in this way would be quick to agree with C. S. Lewis, who noted that those most willing to die for their beliefs are often those most willing to kill for them. To avoid becoming a villain, then, it is best to hold your own beliefs in check with a dash of humor: "I wouldn't take any of it too seriously." Since our great-great-grandchildren are going to be laughing at us, why not join them?

So in a postmodern world it makes good sense to have a twenty-four-hour comedy channel on cable TV. Wryness is the posture of postmodernism—not the self-righteous indignation of a late-modern Ian Malcolm, but rather the ironic "whatever" of a teenager who feels that on the other side nothing is worth getting so worked up over. Alternative rock singer Alanis Morisette's wry song "Ironic" could well be the national anthem of postmodernism—sung, of course, with a wry smile and a sad laugh.

4. Postmodernism highly values subjective experience.

Having dispensed with worldviews and belief systems, what's left? The rocking of a boat, the smell of salt, the warmth of sunlight—"there isn't really anything else," Thorne says. But we shouldn't make the mistake of claiming that subjective experience is Truth. No, that would be transition-zone thinking, more modern than postmodern. For people on the other side, experience is just experience. It's all there is, and "life is wonderful. It's a gift to be alive, to see the sun and breathe the air." For postmoderns, it's better simply to experience experience than to turn it into another theory or universalize it and proclaim it as Truth.

5. For postmoderns, togetherness is a rare, precious, and elusive experience.

Thorne doesn't recommend arguing with Malcolm. In fact, he clearly cherishes the togetherness they feel, having survived an ordeal together: "You see all of us together? That's real. Life is wonderful." In a world where everyone sees things differently, where everyone lives according to differing theories ("Human beings can't help making them," Thorne says), it is far better to practice tolerance and appreciate diversity than to capsize the boat by stirring up controversy.

It is this yearning for togetherness that inspires the oft-heard postmodern motifs of pluralism and tolerance. As D. A. Carson makes so clear, the term *pluralism* can mean many things, from common decency and good manners to a radical intolerance masquerading as tolerance.[6] The latter absurd extreme serves, under the mask of tolerance, to assert elitist formulations like these:

STRATEGY TWELVE A

—"All beliefs are equally valid, unless you actually believe them."

—"All beliefs are equally valid, but only, of course, if you believe them in the wry, ironic way of a postmodern."

—"All beliefs are equally valid, except those that claim to be True (which effectively excludes all beliefs except this one—that is, postmodernism itself)."

In this way postmodernism is the latest in a long series of absurdities. For example, Freudianism says that all beliefs and behaviors flow out of certain psychosexual complexes—all beliefs except Freudianism, of course, and all behaviors except the behavior of expounding Freudianism.

According to evolutionism, all characteristics, including the development of thinking brains, are selected naturally to favor survival—not necessarily the apprehension of truth. This belief suggests that the very organ that conceives of evolution is oriented to produce useful theories but not necessarily true ones. Marxism and Skinnerian behaviorism alike suggest that individual human behaviors are determined, whether by class-struggle or pain-avoidance mechanisms—conveniently excluding the behaviors of the theorists themselves, who speak and write as if their theories were generated in the vacuum of a pure search for truth rather than in the mechanism of their own socioeconomic or intrapersonal dynamics. Radical postmodernism rejects the universal truthfulness of every other belief while assuming its own position as the only universally true one.

In my experience, however, most postmoderns are not really this radical, although they may quickly sound that way when goaded by insensitive Christians castigating them for the abandonment of "absolutes." Really, what most of them want is nothing more or less than the gentleness and noncoerciveness required of wise Christian leaders in 2 Timothy 2:24–25: "The Lord's servant must not quarrel; instead, he must be kind to everyone, able to teach, not resentful. Those who oppose him he must gently instruct, in the hope that God will give them repentance leading them to a knowledge of the truth." (This gentleness informs the rhetorical concerns in Strategy 6, you will recall.) In short, because of their value of togetherness and corresponding fear of disintegration (a wise fear in a world of Jihads, right-wing militias, and ethnic cleansing), postmoderns don't want truth without equal doses of love. (Have I heard that phrase before somewhere?)

CRITIQUING CHRISTIAN CRITIQUES

Many Christian critiques of postmodernism would be improved, I think, by learning a bit more from their subject. The critiques often arise from a modern viewpoint, which seems valid only from the context or standpoint of modernity. Let me point out two common misunderstandings.

Myth 1: Postmoderns don't believe in absolute truth.

The dismissal of absolute truth is an easy misconception to have because this is what postmoderns will say and what the most radical may believe. But I do not think this is what rank-and-file postmoderns mean. When they answer no to the question, Do you believe in absolute truth? this is what I think they really mean: "Well, of course there is absolute truth out there. I don't doubt that. I just doubt your ability, or my own for that matter, to apprehend that truth and comprehend it and remember it and encode it in language and communicate it to others and have them understand it in any absolutely accurate way."

In other words, what postmodern people tend to reject is not absolute truth, but absolute knowledge. And to the degree we seek to defend absolute knowledge, we show ourselves to be defenders not of biblical faith (which repeatedly affirms that we "know in part") but of modern rationalism (which displays an overconfidence about its autonomous powers of knowledge that is hard to overexaggerate).

Having a universe full of absolute truth but a world full of people incapable of grasping and conveying it with absolute accuracy is *almost*—but not exactly—the same as having no absolute truth at all. Failing to see this distinction, many Christians in the current transition zone keep beating the drum of absolute truth, and the harder they beat it, the more primitive and hopelessly

modern they seem. Frankly, I think the term *absolute truth* has out-
lived its usefulness.

Myth 2: Postmoderns don't care about truth.

I believe that postmoderns care about truth so much that they
don't want to pretend a subjective opinion or "view from a point"
is more than it really is. And they care about truth so much that
they question the ability of language to convey it sufficiently.

"Imagine a line of people trying to pass a handful of sand from
one end to the other," the postmodern might suggest. "With each
passing, some sand is lost. Now imagine that the truth is not just
a handful of sand, but rather all the sand on all the beaches of the
world. How can we claim to hold the truth and pass it on, when
our hands not only lose so much but grasp so little?"

Actually, deep down, although they would probably not risk
fighting about it, postmoderns might say that most Christians
don't care about the truth as much as many postmoderns do: "If
Christians prize truth so highly, why can you turn on late-night
cable TV and see a dozen different Christian preachers, with a
dozen different spins on the truth, all proclaiming with apparent
certainty that their version is right and everyone else's is wrong?"
Maybe that tendency to arrogant debate and presumptuous
proclamation is what they don't believe in when they say they
don't believe in truth. If by "truth" we mean honesty, authenticity, and genuineness, all but the most radical will sign on as believers in a heartbeat.

ARE TWO-STAGE CONVERSIONS NECESSARY? —————

Years ago, when I was a college English teacher, a fundamentalist
Christian group took up street preaching on the campus. It was
standard nineteenth-century revivalism, and it tended to draw loud
and raucous crowds. Between classes I would stand at the edge of
the amused circle and listen and occasionally have interesting dialogue with other listeners. But over time I noticed that the content of the preaching shifted from Christianity to conservative
politics. The group, in fact, began organizing conservative political

rallies. This syncretism (a mixture of the gospel with another agenda) bothered me even more than the anachronistic revivalism had, so I scheduled a meeting with one of the street preachers.

"Why are you doing this?" I asked. "Have you lost your faith in the gospel and switched over to trust politics?"

"Oh, no, not at all," the preacher explained. "People are so liberal these days, we've come to realize that before we can convert them to Christ, we have to convert them to conservatism."

The church in the transition zone, I fear, is making a similar mistake when it comes to confronting postmodernism. We can hardly conceive of a postmodern being able to become a Christian without becoming modern first (or immediately after); similarly, we can hardly conceive that our way of seeing Christianity is not the only way, but rather the modern way. If we are to be effective on the other side, we ourselves will have to become less modern and more postmodern—not completely of it, of course, but more completely in it. Eugene Peterson's rendering of Paul's words about becoming all things to all men are poignantly relevant to us, in a world comprising not just Jews and Gentiles, but also moderns and postmoderns: "I didn't take on their way of life. I kept my bearings in Christ—but I entered their world and tried to experience things from their point of view."[7]

Fortunately, more and more Christians are seeking to understand postmodernism before judging it.[8] Years ago Dr. Richard Halverson (who was later to become the chaplain of the U.S. Senate) made a distinction between dogmatism and faith that would be music to postmodernist ears:

> Dogmatism and faith are not identical! Dogmatism is like stone. Faith is like soil.
>
> Dogmatism refuses to admit doubt. Faith often struggles with doubt.
>
> Dogmatism is brittle ... cracks under pressure. Faith is resilient, malleable and teachable. Dogmatism is defensive ... stereotyped ... static. Faith rests ... but it is never smug, pat or complacent.
>
> Dogmatism is a closed system. Faith is open to reason.

STRATEGY TWELVE A

Dogmatism is a tunnel. Faith is a mountain peak.

Dogmatism fills one with pride. Faith inspires awe and reverence.

Dogmatism insists on propositions. Faith knows Christ.

Dogmatism generates bigotry. Faith stimulates understanding.[9]

It is this kind of faith that will help us understand postmodernism. And it is this kind of faith that postmoderns can accept—no, are attracted to—no, are dying for.

A PERSONAL WORD

One day not long ago, a woman who was a fairly new Christian came to see me in my office. She had developed into one of the best Sunday school teachers in our church; the children relished her energy, enthusiasm, love, and creativity. She said, "Brian, I think we have a problem. I think I believe something different from the other teachers. I don't want to cause trouble, so I thought I should talk to you about it."

I thanked her for this uncommon courtesy and asked her what the problem was. She replied, "I think most of the teachers here believe that Jesus is the only way. I have a real problem with that."

Her problem was a classic postmodern dilemma. Resisting the temptation to address the issue of pluralism versus the uniqueness of Christ, I asked another question: "Why is this a problem for you?"

Her answer illustrates one of the delightful paradoxes of postmodernism: "My two best friends are not Christians. There is nothing I want more in my life than for them to discover what I've discovered these last few years. But if I tell them that I believe they are going to hell because they don't believe in Jesus, they will never listen to another word I have to say."

Do you see the irony? More important, do you feel her dilemma, and mine as her pastor? If you do, you are well on your way to understanding what it means to be a Christian in a postmodern world.

Enter the Postmodern World—Part B: Engage It

*Engage postmodernism,
and maximize the
opportunities it presents.*

Many see postmodernism as a threat while others see it as an exciting opportunity. Both are right. D. A. Carson acknowledges,

> In my most somber moods I sometimes wonder if the ugly face of what I refer to as philosophical pluralism is the most dangerous threat to the gospel since the rise of the gnostic heresy in the second century, and for some of the same reasons. . . . In a happier frame I suspect that . . . postmodernism is proving rather successful at undermining the extraordinary hubris of modernism, and no thoughtful Christian can be entirely sad about that.[1]

Because others, like Carson, have warned us of the "ugly face," I will focus here on the brighter side. For Christian innovators eager to build the new church, the opportunities presented by postmodernism are downright exciting. So I come here to engage postmodernism, not to bury it.

Before us lies a new world—a world nearly empty spiritually, which makes it hungry and thirsty for good spiritual bread and wine. It is a world hostile to dogmatism but ready to be sown with good seeds of vibrant, living faith. If we as Christians do not fill the need, someone else will. An article in *NetFax* highlighted this opportunity:

The March issue of *Swing*, a new magazine targeted at people in their twenties, is focused on this search and the headline of the cover screams "SPIRITUALITY RETURNS." In this pluralistic 21st century world, the search for spirituality takes many forms and the articles range from the Zen based coaching and play of the incredible 1995–1996 Chicago Bulls to the hottest healers in Hollywood and from the Hare Krishnas punk rockers to wayward young Jews rediscovering the power of observance and their faith. According to the editorial, in a recent survey of twentysomethings finding spiritual fulfillment was ranked more important than achieving financial success.[2]

True, we will have to change in order to seize the opportunity, but I believe that with God's help, the challenge will do us good. Here are some ideas for maximizing the opportunity.

OPPORTUNITY MAXIMIZERS

1. We have to distinguish between genuine Christianity and our (individual and various culture-encoded) versions of it.

As I have already stated in these pages, I believe our modern version of Christianity won't work on the other side, any more than a software program will work on an incompatible platform. Postmodern software won't read, much less run, our data if they are encrypted in archaic modern code.

Now, some of you are wondering whether I actually mean what I am saying. In good postmodern fashion I will answer that I mean what I am saying, but maybe not what you think I'm saying. What I mean to say could be expressed in a number of aphorisms, from which you can pick the easiest for you to work with.

A. I believe Christianity is true, but I do not believe that my version (or yours, for that matter) of the Faith is completely true. (In other words, I believe that all versions are incomplete in some ways, weighed down with extra baggage, and marred by impurities, biases, misconceptions, and gaps.)

B. I believe Jesus is true, but I don't believe Christianity in any of our versions is true. (In other words, we know in part and prophesy in part; we have not yet reached that unity and maturity of faith and knowledge that will come when we know as we are known.)

C. I believe there is no completely true version of Christianity anywhere except, of course, in the mind of God. (In other words, incompleteness and error are part of the reality of being human.)

These acknowledgments remove huge barriers to postmoderns, who are sensitive to overstatements that nudge faith toward dogmatism.

2. We need to see truth and goodness where they exist in postmodernism.

This statement carries a certain irony for the sensitive reader, but an appropriate irony, I think. Even though many postmoderns would feel uncomfortable talking about truth and defining goodness, as Christians we should be quick to affirm the following postmodern insights and qualities wherever they appear:

A. *An Appropriate Humility:* The know-it-all arrogance of the modern world feels chastened in postmodernism. People are prone to walk more humbly. Expressing this humility in an enchanting lyric, postmodern Christian songwriter Bruce Cockburn says: "All these years of thinking / Ended up like this, / In front of all this beauty / Understanding nothing."[3] (The modern version would have read, " . . . in front of all this matter / controlling everything.")

B. *A Healthy Skepticism:* Jesus himself said to "consider carefully what you hear,"[4] and postmoderns agree: You can't believe everything you hear. The experts especially should be doubted, in the same way that Jesus doubted the Pharisees.

C. *A Thirst for Spirituality:* Gone with the passing of the modern world is its spiritless empiricism. Because people experience spirituality, that's all the evidence needed to conclude that spirituality is real and worthy of exploration.

D. *An Openness to Faith:* Because knowledge is a luxury beyond our means, faith is the best we can hope for. What an opportunity! Faith hasn't encountered openness like this in several hundred years.

E. A Congenial Tolerance: Such tolerance became too rare in the contentious modern world, but it is probably the prime directive of the postmodern. Whom would you rather live next to—a tolerant postmodern, or a judgmental, angry evangelist? (Maybe more of us can promote a rarer option, the tolerant evangelist!) Many Christians see this tolerance as an obstacle, but Mike Regele has it right when he sees fantastic opportunity in postmodernism for telling the "grand story" of the gospel:

> It will not be a barrier to our culture if we present it as the great story. In a postmodern world, there is a story for every occasion. It is only a barrier when we are miffed that we have to take our place in the marketplace of stories, enjoying no favored position. For example, when we continually make a big issue out of school prayer, we are perceived as trying to coerce people. We must let these issues go. If we can't let them go, we will fail in our mission. If we can, the opportunity to proclaim again the story of Jesus, and the hope of life that is in him alone, will open before us. It is the unsurpassable story. No other story answers the question, What is life? or the question, Where is meaning to be found?[5]

F. A Limited Relativism: I am not recommending that we affirm absolute relativism (which is logically an absurdity), but rather honest, limited relativism. Postmoderns have been reared under the post-Einsteinian, quantum knowledge that even time and space are not absolute. So they are justly skeptical of absolutist claims and understandably sensitive to moral ambiguities, including some found in the Bible. Is it absolutely wrong to kill your own child? (Abraham was commanded to do so.) Is it absolutely wrong to worship in an idol's temple? (Naaman was given permission to do so.) Is it absolutely wrong to visit a prostitute? (Hosea was commanded to do so.) Is it absolutely wrong to have more than one wife? (Many good Bible characters had such.) Is it absolutely wrong to have slaves? (Then why does the Bible regulate rather than categorically forbid slavery?)

Dare we acknowledge that many moral issues are relative to their situation—under God? Perhaps if we were more honest

STRATEGY TWELVE B

about the number of moral ambiguities in the Bible and in life, non-Christian postmoderns would be more open to some of our claims of universal (a term I think would be better understood than "absolute") truth.

3. We need to magnify the importance of faith.

Faith was an embarrassment in the modern world. It is what you had to settle for when you couldn't have scientific certainty. In the postmodern world, it seems, everyone lives by faith. No one I know of understands this better than Lesslie Newbigin. In *Proper Confidence: Faith, Doubt, and Certainty in Christian Discipleship,*[6] Newbigin retraces our modern love affair with the critical methods of rationalism in a lust for scientific certainty. From Descartes through Kant to Neitzsche, modern thinkers have been striving to find a ground of certainty without any recourse to faith.

But the love affair has ended somewhat bitterly after all these years, Newbigin says, in nihilism. Scientific certainty of the kind we find in mathematics breaks down when we bring it from abstraction and theory to real life. Ultimate, unshakable, noncontingent certainty is surely available to God, and perhaps to the angels, but part of our human predicament, postmoderns acknowledge, is the gap between our aspiration for absolute, autonomous knowledge and our ability to attain it. (One can't help but think of Eve's grasp for the forbidden fruit of knowledge in Genesis, or the Preacher's conclusion in Ecclesiastes 3:11: "He has also set eternity in the hearts of men; yet they cannot fathom what God has done from beginning to end.")

Now—nudged along by postmodern thinkers like Michael Polanyi, the late-modern scientists of the new physics, and ancient lights like the great Augustine—we find ourselves returning to Augustine's realization: "I believe in order to understand." In other words, there is no certainty apart from faith, and the only kind of understanding possible for us humans grows in the environment of faith. The issue, then, isn't faith versus certainty any more, but rather good faith versus bad faith. And that issue is good ground to explore with our postmodern neighbors (an exploration I have put myself to in my second book, *Finding Faith* [Zondervan, 1999]).

4. We ought to be more fair.

I recently read this statement in an article written by a Christian thinker whom I respect and generally enjoy reading: "Pastors may have admirable intentions and the highest motives, but they may still, in the end, inadvertently dishonor the Lord and distort his gospel. The megachurch movement, for example, is a case in point." His first sentence raises a valid point. The second sentence offers a mega-generalization that glibly obscures whatever truth may pertain: What are the specific things that raise his concern? What is the range of his experience in megachurches that warrants making such a generalization?

Whether this writer is technically right or wrong, in the postmodern world he is being grossly unfair. Why? Because he is applying a scrutiny to someone else that he has not applied to himself. (At least, I hope he hasn't. Otherwise, he is claiming to be authorized to cast the first stone, having proven himself to have not only the best intentions and purest motives, but also a distortion-free version of the gospel.) We (and I include me) are always the last to see our own faults.

In other words, we need to be more careful about applying a degree of scrutiny to others (other Christians, non-Christians, postmoderns, "the world," megachurches, or whomever) that we can not ourselves withstand. This is, of course, nothing more than Jesus' splinter-and-beam principle coming up once again (Matthew 7:3–5).

This desire to be fair—to treat others no more harshly than one treats oneself or wants others to treat oneself—is precious to postmoderns. But it imposes a heavy burden and requires much hard work and leaves one too often feeling silly or hypocritical. A corollary to this fairness principle, as we saw in an earlier chapter, is to stop comparing "our" best examples with "their" worst.

5. We need to be more experiential.

Christians have been arguing for several decades about how experiential faith should be, with "charismatics" voting for experience and everybody else voting for something else (in various combinations of tradition, doctrine, reason, and discipline). But unfor-

STRATEGY TWELVE B

tunately, all sides seem to lose out on the other side, for at least four reasons: (a) What passes for Christian "experience" often seems so hyped, faked, put on, or inflated as to turn postmoderns off rather than on; (b) some of our more extreme experiences appear desperate, manic, or otherwise pathological rather than attractive; (c) our experience too often appears to be the result of manipulation or coercion by authority figures such as pastors, and postmoderns hold all coercion suspect; (d) the obvious alternative, a rational nonexperiential faith, comes off as quite boring to postmoderns, who are waiting for a moving, substantial experience, not just vaporous principles or concepts.

The kind of experience we need more of is honest, unforced, and unhyped experience: honest feeling, uncensored, unedited, based on reflection, and honestly shared with others in stories. These stories can be about the experience of the absence of God as well as his presence, about anger as well as affection, failures as well as victories, disappointments as well as miracles. They can be either major breakthroughs or what Cockburn calls little "rumors of glory." The Bible offers many examples of this naive honesty about experience, especially with Jesus: "My soul is overwhelmed with sorrow ... " and "My God, my God, why ...?"[7]

6. We need to address the postmoderns' existential predicament.

It's tough living as a postmodern. It's tough living without certainty. It's a burden having to relativize nearly everything, including one's own beliefs. How does one make decisions? How does one live through a Wednesday, conduct a marriage, raise kids, endure humiliations and setbacks, or rebound from depressions? How does one get traction in a weightless world? We can help if we can address these predicaments.

So far, we have not done well in this regard. For example, we hear postmoderns say they don't believe in truth, so we react by quoting John 14:6, implying that if you don't believe in truth, you can't believe in Jesus, who said, "I am the way and the truth and the life." This implication is not especially helpful and, in fact, may miss a wonderful opportunity. In typical modern fashion, we see these as three discrete items—way, truth, life—and as good moderns we are especially comfortable with the middle item, probably infusing the word with abstract, doctrinal connotations. In context, however, consider that Jesus may have been using a technique of Hebrew parallelism, suggesting "way–truth–life" as three ways of saying the same thing.

If that's the case, this is exactly what postmoderns need. They need an integrated "way–truth–life" that is relational, not just conceptual; experiential, not theoretical; addressed to the will ("follow me") not just the mind ("assent to this formulation as absolutely true"). Jesus' words in John 7:17 take on a fresh ring in this light: "If anyone chooses to do God's will, he will find out whether my teaching comes from God." In other words, it is in the midst of following the way, of living the life, that one finds the truth. This approach can help postmoderns in their predicament of needing truth, yet being suspicious of those who claim to "have" it. Asking them to assent to a formulation that they have no confidence in won't help them. We can do better!

7. We need to listen to the postmoderns' stories.

Perhaps the reason that I seem so sympathetic to postmoderns, despite having been born into the late modern world, is that I have really listened to my postmodern friends. I think of a buddy of mine back in graduate school. He was a true postmodern, doing his doctorate in deconstructionist literary criticism. He had a brilliant mind and a sensitive spirit. One day as we stood together in a checkout line in a store, he said, out of the blue, with a sincerity that still brings tears to my eyes, "Brian, it must be nice to have faith."

I said, "Yeah, but it's not easy sometimes."

And he replied, "Not having faith isn't so easy either."

There were stories behind those words, and I heard a few. I only wish I would have listened to more.

8. We need to tell our stories.

In the modern world we could wield a proposition like a sword, a concept like a hammer. In the postmodern world we have to hold a mystery like a lover, and a story like a child.

We need to tell our own stories: unedited, unsanitized, rough and lumpy, not squeezed into a formula. Should we be cross with postmoderns for feeling that stories are the best conveyers of truth? Looking at the Bible, it appears that God might be postmodern in this respect too!

In part, this means being more honest—with ourselves and with postmoderns. Our doubts, failures, fears, problems, embarrassments, and confessions have tremendous apologetic and pastoral value in a postmodern world. They illustrate "truth" in its postmodern form of honesty, authenticity, transparency.

9. We need to address issues we have never even thought about before.

In chapter 6 I recounted my experience of addressing some Chinese visiting scholars. I can't forget another bright "post-doc" who asked me this question that night: "Sir, I have been trying to read the Bible. But I find it very difficult, and I think it is driving me farther from God, not closer. Maybe you can help me. I read that God told the Jewish people to kill all non-Jewish people in a certain area. I realize that if I had lived in that area, God would have told them to kill me, since I am Asian, not Jewish. This makes me feel more alienated from this Jewish God, like he hates me and is prejudiced against me. How am I to respond to this problem?"

What would you say to this man? Although I had never considered that question before (even though I also, being of Scottish descent, am no more Jewish than he), immediately it struck me: Yes, this is an important issue! I can't dodge it or patch over it with a cliché, an easy answer that doesn't really fit. (If you're wondering what I said, I can't remember. I think I told him, "I'm sorry, I don't know.")

10. We need to avoid coercion and pressure.

Coercion and pressure were the hallmarks of nineteenth-century revivalism, and with good reason. The preacher of that day was addressing people who by and large knew the Christian gospel but were willfully rebelling against it. Their stubborn wills needed direct confrontation: Their message might aptly have been expressed, "Turn or burn!"

Do you see how different our current situation is? Do you see how grossly inappropriate "turn or burn" is now? (Or should we put it, "You capitulate or we'll legislate"?) I believe our situation today is much like that in Matthew 9:36, where Jesus looked with compassion at the multitudes wandering as sheep without a shepherd, doing the best they could with what they had. Yes, like Jesus, we can find a place for strong language—he used it with the highly religious big guys who should have known better. But for the wandering sheep, gentleness was required. Our event- and decision-oriented approach to conversion may be a remnant of revivalism; in the postmodern world we seem to be experiencing a pendulum swing toward a process orientation. Although this is very different, it seems fitting and seems to be working.

11. We need to see the postmoderns in here, out there, and everywhere.

It is not just in evangelizing non-Christians that we meet postmoderns. We also meet them in church. They are not just other people's sons and daughters, but also our own. They are not just the younger generation; many older people have also become postmodern. They are not just a minority; soon old-fashioned moderns will be the minority, like those farmers who remain to till the fields when everyone else has moved to the city and suburbs.

Postmoderns are not just Americans or even Westerners; they are also Chinese, Africans, Eastern Europeans, and Latinos. And they obviously are not just Christians, or even nominal Christians. Members of every religion are being influenced by postmodernism. I was in a refugee shelter in Regensburg, Germany, and met a winsome young Afghan woman, a devout Muslim, but a postmodern if ever there was one: "There is only one God, and all religions lead to God," she said.

How can postmodernism be as ubiquitous as Coca-Cola and McDonald's? Because all over the world we are sharing the same formative experiences: pluralization (being confronted by many different beliefs, in person and through the media), higher education (which exposes us to other cultures and ways of thinking, across barriers of geography, class, and time), hypocrisy (each -ism has its share of well-publicized scandals in high places, which serve to weaken confidence in and loyalty to all traditions and institutions), revolutions and counter-revolutions (which weaken faith in ideologies), the breakdown of families (through migration, urbanization, divorce, etc., thus weakening traditional bonds), and so much more.

12. **We must rely more than ever on art, music, literature, and drama to communicate our message.**

Dennis Haack of Ransom Fellowship says it well:

> Story, song, and image can be used as points of contact to explore the big issues of life without compromising the integrity of the gospel. Popular culture (TV, film, pop music), the very heart of the postmodern ethos, can become the beginning point for exploring the claims of Christ, and thus serve as the postmodern equivalent of the Athenian altar to an unknown god. Modernity required an apologetic that was essentially rational; a postmodern apologetic needs to be essentially rooted in glory, with a greater emphasis on art, narrative, and image (without for a moment being anything less than rational).[8]

Who could have guessed that post-Christian, postmodern France would see in the 1990s a phenomenon like the Taize movement, in which thousands of young people from the unchurched majority as well as the churched minority would gather for days on end to hear deeply spiritual, meditative worship music rooted in Scripture? Or who could have predicted the revival of interest in Gregorian chant evidenced by a Spanish CD that became a popular best-seller around the world?

Closer to home, in my own church, almost every year I present a series of sermons called "God in the Movies." I show clips of popular movies that contain spiritually relevant themes, linking them to passages of Scripture that we explore in depth. It's relatively common for preachers like me to use examples of popular culture as disdainful evidence of the decadence of contemporary society, but the key to this series is that I almost never do that; instead, I look for moments of "glory" in the films and trace that glory to its source in the Creator. Each year I am amazed by the response; film has become, like music, a kind of universal language, and people appreciate it when we take the time to learn their culture and exegete it with respect, not disdain.

Similarly, like thousands of other churches, my congregation has been inspired by Willow Creek's example in the use of drama. On occasion we have enjoyed liturgical dance as an expression of worship, and postmodern people respond. Haack is right: We should not be less than rational, but we must increasingly be more, augmenting the rational with the aesthetic. One wonders, How could such a beautiful message of incarnation be faithfully told without such artistic embodiment?

13. We must believe that the Holy Spirit is out there at work already.

The Chinese Christian leader Ni To-sheng (Watchman Nee) articulated an approach to evangelism that will help us a great deal:

> I always believe that the Holy Spirit is upon a person when I preach to that person. I do not mean that the Spirit is within the hearts of unbelievers, but that He is outside. What is He doing? He is waiting, waiting to bring Christ into their hearts. He is like the light. Open the window-shutters even a little, and it will flood in and illuminate the interior. Let there be a cry from the heart to God, and at that moment the Spirit will enter and begin His transforming work of conviction and repentance and faith.
>
> Perhaps the biggest condition for success in bringing people to Christ is to remember that the same Holy Spirit, who came to our help in the hour of darkness, is at hand waiting to enter and illumine their hearts also, and to make good the work of salvation to which, in crying to God, they have opened the door.[9]

True, maybe the Holy Spirit will work in ways and places we will not easily recognize. But knowing that Jesus often worked in unexpected ways,[10] should we really be surprised? My wife, who works as a consultant with "secular" CEOs, has many stories of spiritual openness in unexpected places. Recently she was discussing spiritual matters with one bright entrepreneur, who said, "There's a lot of spirituality going on out here. It's just that we're doing it without you guys"—meaning without the church. Maybe we need to simply relax, open our eyes to see what God is doing "out there," and then try to cooperate.

14. We must become seekers again.

The term *seeker* has entered our vocabulary in recent years to describe the as-yet-unconverted who are seeking Christ, gradually responding to the prevenient grace and work of God's Spirit upon them, as Ni To-sheng put it. *Seeker* is a good term, but if it leads the rest of us to consider ourselves "finders" and therefore "nonseekers," it has a sad side effect. If we can present ourselves to our postmodern neighbors not as an exclusive inner circle of "in the know" finders but rather as seekers ourselves—people on the path, folks who don't have all the answers but who feel they are genuinely onto something—if we can do that, then the seekers around us will feel a kinship with us and many will join us on the path. They will very likely become part of our community before they commit to our beliefs, and their conversions will often be so process-oriented that the moment of regeneration will be difficult or impossible to identify. But gradually they will hear through us the "follow me" of Jesus Christ, and they will say, "I will follow."

15. We must reassert the value of community and rekindle the experience of it.

I believe Lesslie Newbigin is right when he asserts that the greatest apologetic for the gospel is and always has been a community that actually lives by the gospel.

> I confess that I have come to feel that the primary reality of which we have to take account in seeking for a Christian impact on public life is the Christian congregation. How is it possible that the gospel should be credible, that people should come to believe that the power which has the last word in human affairs is represented by a man hanging on a cross? I am suggesting that the only answer, the only hermeneutic of

the gospel, is a congregation of men and women who believe it and live by it.... [E]vangelistic campaigns, distribution of Bibles and Christian literature, conferences, and even books such as this one . . . are all secondary, and . . . they have power to accomplish their purpose only as they are rooted in and lead back to a believing community. Jesus . . . did not write a book but formed a community.[11]

Newbigin is simply reaffirming Jesus' own promise: Our love for one another, our visible demonstration of living community, will prove both our legitimacy and his. This is truer than ever in a community-starved postmodern culture, where the pendulum has swung to extreme individualism, isolation, and loneliness.

ODDVILLE

I can't help but think in this regard of a bizarre TV show of the late nineties on the "postmodern channel"—MTV. The show, aptly called *Oddville*, featured the oddest assortment of real people imaginable. They would come on the show to demonstrate their offbeat "talents"—from identifying animal crackers with the tongue to wearing a beard of honeybees to imitating dogs to cracking joints to making grotesque faces. Each guest would then sit on a long couch (next to a near-catatonic fellow who simply sat there each day as stiff as a mannequin, saying nothing) to observe and applaud the next offbeat guest. With typical postmodern irony, the show represented, I think, a wry longing for community, for a place in this world of celebrities and superstars and supermodels where the rest of us—in all our oddness—are accepted, applauded, and appreciated.

Another genre of show on MTV illustrates a similar dream— the Real World and Road Rules series, where real people (not actors) simply have to live together for six months, get along, work together, in spite of their diversity, hoping to forge some sort of community in which viewers can vicariously participate.

Granted, our churches too often have unwanted Oddville characteristics, but isn't that the point? The church is to be a place in this world for the "poor, the crippled, the blind and the lame"

STRATEGY TWELVE B

(Luke 14:21), a place of real acceptance and love, where "the least of these" have importance, where you don't have to be a star to be valued, where your oddness (or sin) won't exclude you. Isn't the reality of a community of real people (odd people, people on the road, real world people)—people authentically loving one another—isn't that the one great apologetic without which all other apologetics taste flat and dry? And isn't this even more true in postmodern, community-poor times like today and tomorrow?

We should be forewarned at this juncture, because postmodernism may present the greatest threat to unity (and therefore community) faced by the Christian church and by individual congregations in our lifetimes. Polarization over postmodernism may resurrect, reconfigure, and amplify the old furies between fundamentalists and liberals of the late modern era. If that's the case, we have a tough challenge ahead of us. We know that what Jesus said follows if we love one another, if our salt remains salty and our light bright; we must repeatedly remind ourselves of the consequences that follow if we *don't* love one another, if we lose our saltiness, if our light is obscured by the lampshade of division. At the very least, we all, conservatives and liberals, need to learn to disagree more agreeably, to show due diligence in our call to "keep the unity of the Spirit through the bond of peace" (Ephesians 4:3).

ACTION-REACTION

*B*ut maybe we must learn even more than that. If liberalism is seen as a selling out to modernism or postmodernism (which it may well be), then it would make sense to anticipate a conservative reaction to the postmodern revolution. And there are plenty of signs, in America at least, of that kind of reaction taking shape. To those conservatives, what I am suggesting in this chapter (and this whole book) must seem like the most shameless kind of compromise, defeat, and surrender—an ill-advised walk on the slippery slope. Are they right? Or is it possible that both liberals and conservatives will need to be called to a third alternative, to leave their entrenched positions and learn something from one another, to become something new together in the new world?

Nancey Murphy explores this possibility very articulately in *Beyond Liberalism and Fundamentalism*. She says,

> The differences between liberal and conservative theologies ... are less significant than those between modern thinkers of all sorts and those who have adopted the standpoint of a new intellectual world in the making, which I label Anglo-American postmodernity.... Yet I make the claim, perhaps startling to some, that this revolution offers hope for a rapprochement between Christians of the left and right. Constructive dialogue is already taking place between postliberals and "postmodern evangelicals."[12]

The postmodern revolution, Murphy suggests, presents a new set of questions and challenges to Christian thinkers both liberal and conservative. These new questions and challenges invite both sides to simply walk away from the old arguments of modernity, neither side winning or losing. Then both sides can join together, bringing their diverse perspectives and strengths gained during modernity, to address the new questions, challenges, and opportunities on the other side. (It makes me think of the Vietnam war. Who won it? Who lost? Didn't everyone eventually just lose interest, as the old Cold War ended, and the world changed?)

In this transition zone, both liberals and conservatives are divided in their responses to postmodernity. Some fear it. Others welcome it. Who's right?

Remember the old image of a dog barking up the wrong tree? Well, what if you have two dogs, or two packs of dogs, and one pack is barking up one tree, and the other is barking up the other? Is one pack wrong and the other right? Maybe. But maybe there's something worth barking at up both trees. Maybe that is the case here. There is much to fear in postmodernism. Selling out to it is not the answer—my conservative friends are right about that. But am I being presumptuous to suggest that there is something up the other tree, too? Is it not possible—in fact desirable, even necessary—to reject the alternative of selling out to postmodernism

STRATEGY TWELVE B

and at the same time to reject the opposite alternative of railing against it and attempting to remain aloof from it? Is it not possible to enter postmodernism incarnationally, as Jesus entered our world, learning its language, telling parables that make sense in its context, feeling its pain, understanding its dreams, loving its people, thoroughly in it while not being of it? Again, might there be something up both trees after all?

And speaking of trees, maybe our different reactions to postmodernism reflect the different roles we play in the family tree of faith. Maybe you're a root, designed to hold on, to be immovable, deep, even isolated from the latest winds of change. Maybe you're a trunk, depended on to sway only a little, to remain steadfast and strong, absorbing the shock of wind and storm, serving as a conduit between roots and branches (because both need each other in spite of their differences). And maybe I'm a branch, or a leaf far out on a limb, intended to feel the changing breezes. If that's the case, then I have a role to play, too; it's out on the green edge of things that new growth happens and solar energy is harnessed. One tree, many functions—a good metaphor for us, don't you think?

MY OWN ROOTS

*P*ostmodernism was spawned in the field of literary criticism, the field in which I did my graduate study. It was just hitting the scholarly world as I entered graduate school, but it was known then as *deconstructionism* (a term as hard to explain as *postmodernism*).

If you are upset with me because of this chapter, you might be tempted to say to me, "See, you were influenced by your worldly environment. You became 'of the world' instead of remaining different while 'in the world.'" And if you say that, I must warn you that you are talking like a postmodern, claiming that my ability to see clearly and think objectively is swayed by the sociology of the group I choose as my context. (Do you have the same kind of problem?)

Another way to see it would be to say that perhaps God "led me" (a young man with a strong evangelical Christian heritage and a deeply personal Christian commitment) into graduate school in that field at that time for this very purpose: to sensitize me to issues on the other side of this huge transition we have been born into, and to equip me to somehow be of some small help.

A comparison to Moses is so grandiose as to be avoided by a wise writer. But Moses offers one type of precedent in that God used "the Egyptians" to educate one of his servants at an opportune time in opportune ways to fulfill a valuable role.

Moses brings another image to mind. The changes we face as the church—these turbulent changes and raging crosscurrents: Perhaps they are our Red Sea. Perhaps, like the ancient Jewish refugees, we are terrified, caught between a world that is dying and another waiting to be born, grumbling about going back to the good old days in the fading modern world, waiting for a Moses to raise his rod in faith and show us there is a way ahead, a way through . . . to the other side.

There won't be a single Moses helping us through these waters. No, there will be many. It is my hope that these pages have located a few of them and sparked them with the courage to help lead the way into the church on the other side.

12c

Enter the Postmodern World—Part C: Get Ready for Revolution

Prepare to de-bug your faith from the viruses of modernity.

*T*heologian/philosopher/futurist Len Sweet says that before we talk about *re*-ing the church, we must *de*-it. Let me paraphrase him using a computer analogy. Before we set ourselves to re-boot the new church on the other side, we must be sure to de-bug it of the viruses it picked up during modernity.

Do you understand how significant that statement is? Do you have a feeling for what it would mean for us to de-bug our churches, our theology, our preaching—to filter out modern viruses? That kind of virus scan won't be easy, and it won't happen overnight—which frustrates us modern Americans, partial as we are to quick fixes. We like to identify the problem at 9:15 A.M., understand it by our 10:30 coffee break, design a solution over lunch, implement the solution at 1:05 P.M., and go home at 5:15 with the problem solved.

What if the postmodern transition is a problem that we won't solve, that our children won't solve, that our grandchildren won't solve? What if the important work of "de-modernizing" the faith will take our whole lifetime, and what if the best gift we bequeath to our children will be space, freedom, permission, opportunity, and encouragement . . . to offer their world a substantially de-bugged Christianity that can "run" in the new matrix?

What if the postmodern transition is not a *problem* at all, but a stage in the ongoing adventure of the coming of the kingdom of God? What if it is less a problem than the end of a problem, if we could just see it accurately?

What if this transition, far from being a problem, is actually a once-in-a-millennium opportunity to do some very creative and exciting and historic work? What if, just as the great Protestant reformers had to scan out medieval viruses, we have the opportunity to scan out modern ones?

ENLIGHTENED ABOUT THE ENLIGHTENMENT

To do this de-ing, we will have to become "enlightened about the Enlightenment" (a philosophical movement of the eighteenth century whose rationalism, empiricism, naturalism, and secularism became the backbone of modernity). The playful phrase "enlightened about the Enlightenment" comes from postmodern philosopher/celebrity Jacques Derrida. John Caputo and Michael Scanlon gave the context for this memorable Derrida-ism, which was uttered during a conference they hosted.

> ... while everyone we invited to this conference was deferential toward the word "religion," most of them were abusive toward the word "postmodernism." Derrida would describe himself not as a postmodern, but as a man of the Enlightenment, albeit of a *new* Enlightenment, one that is enlightened about the Enlightenment and resists letting the spirit of the Enlightenment freeze over into dogma. Derrida seeks an Enlightenment "of our time," here and now, in the sprawling wealth and bottomless poverty, in the uncontainable plurality and virtual reality of this very late-modern, high-tech, televangelist, free-market, multi-media, millennial fin de siècle, this time of need and greed, in which the "certainties and axioms" of the *old* Enlightenment require reconsideration, translation, and transformation.

Later, they explained why they felt this de-bugging of modernity as epitomized by the Enlightenment is so important, especially to people of faith:

STRATEGY TWELVE C

... one way to think of the effect we were trying to provoke in this conference is to imagine its participants as engaged in the common pursuit of pushing past the constraints of this old, methodologically constricted, less enlightened, strait and narrow Enlightenment, which found it necessary to cast "reason" and "religion" in mortal opposition. We sought to seize the contemporary moment which has loosened the grip of the old Enlightenment, questioned its intimidating authority, complained about the exclusionary force of its certainties and axioms (among which *secularism* has enjoyed pride of place), and thereby made some room for a religious discourse and restored the voice of a religious imagination, the Enlightenment ... having chased away one ghost too many. Our wager was, the more enlightened we get about Enlightenment, the more likely religion is to get a word in edgewise.[1]

If Caputo and Scanlon are right—and I believe they are—it is well worth our time and energy to reflect on modernity (the culture born of the eighteenth-century Enlightenment) and its constraints so that we can push beyond them, de-bunking them and de-bugging our faith of them. If we try to sidestep this work, we will be like a doctor performing a faulty blood transfusion. We will take the old blood out—and then put it right back, viruses and all.

SEVEN BUGS

So, if we were to perform a virus scan on our faith, what modern viruses would we look for? Let me suggest seven of the most common and insidious:

1. The Conquest and Control Virus

If we mark modernity's birth at roughly 1500 A.D. (a nice round number around which an amazing number of world-changing discoveries, trends, and inventions clustered, which together reached their full flowering in the Enlightenment), and if we remember a little poem we learned about Columbus sailing the ocean blue in 1492, it is no surprise that modernity has been an era of conquest. Columbus was followed by the "conquistadors," Europeans who began conquering the world with their culture, languages, economy, and religion. What has been conquered must then be controlled, of course, which led to European imperialism, one of the main stories of modernity. How does this affect us as Christians, you ask? Let me respond with a few questions.

Q: What do we Christians often call our evangelistic initiatives?

A: Crusades.

Q: What term do many Christians use to describe evangelism?

A: Winning people for Christ, or "soul winning."

Q: How do many Christians describe their social activism?

A: Culture wars, "taking" America for Christ, etc.

What happens to a culture after five centuries of conquest and control? Might that culture become fatigued with conquest and control and look for other ways to live and act other than by conquering and controlling? Might conservation and collaboration replace conquest and competition, and might empowerment replace control? Can we imagine an approach to evangelism that is not carried out in the spirit of conquest, and styles of spiritual leadership that are not about control? Can we imagine an approach to dealing with other world religions that would differ from the imperialistic patterns of modernity?

2. The Mechanistic Virus

Modernity was the age of the machine. Remember, there had never been a complex machine in the history of the world (maybe the universe?) until the modern era. Enamored as we are of complex machines, and amazed as we are by the mechanical laws of physics that were discovered in the early modern era, it's no wonder that machine imagery has dominated all of our lives. For us, as we view the universe as a great machine, who else would God become but the Great Modern Machine Operator? And what would Christian growth become but a mechanistic, linear, assembly-line process? (After all, soul development must be akin to automotive assembly, right?) What are many seminaries and youth programs and church strategic plans, if not blueprints for the mechanization of spiritual growth, so that Christians can be mass produced (in order to spread and conquer the world, of course)?

If a culture spends five hundred years pursuing the dream of mechanization, and largely succeeds, so that human beings generally feel like little machines in bigger machines, do you think that mechanistic thinking might lose some of its luster? But after decades and decades of mechanistic thinking about spiritual growth, church life, and theological education, do you think we will be able to remember any approaches other than a mechanistic ones? If people indeed grow sick of mechanistic approaches to matters of the heart and spirit, where will we go to find new, post-mechanistic ways of thinking? Certainly not to the engineers, I would think—but maybe to the artists . . . or farmers?

3. The Objective/Analytic/Reductionist Virus

In modernity we became obsessed with a few of our mental capacities (while letting other unfavored capacities atrophy). For example, we felt that we could be sovereign, unbiased, autonomous, knowing subjects, rendering the world around us into objects . . . and rendering our knowledge cleanly objective. In addition, we loved to break down wholes into their constituent parts, or effects into their causes. Then, after dismantling everything else into little parts or causes, we found ourselves the biggest thing left in the universe—a pleasant identity for our egos, at least. And as big, objective, analytical knowers ("we think, therefore we are"), we found ourselves in a position to critique everyone and everything else, reducing it to "nothing but"—nothing but a product of evolution, nothing but an example of class struggle, nothing but an Oedipus complex, whatever.

This kind of thinking didn't stay put in the laboratory or university, however. For example, what did our churches become in modernity but places of Bible exposition (aka objective textual analysis)? What was the ticket to spiritual leadership if not Bible scholarship (that is, credentials certifying our competence at applying modern analytical tools to Bible study)? If our churches leaned to the liberal side, we tended to reduce the Bible to nothing but myths, and if they leaned to the conservative, we tended to reduce it to nothing but propositions, principles, abstractions, doctrines.

Can you see how for maybe four hundred years this could remain interesting and engaging, but after five hundred, our culture would be ready for a new approach . . . something less reductionistic, something more holistic and maybe even mysterious?

4. The Secular/Scientific Virus

One of the signs of the postmodern revolution is the re-dignifying of the word *spiritual*. In modernity nobody wanted to be spiritual; people wanted to be scientific, objective, reasonable, rational . . . not *spiritual*. These days (and many people complain about this, but I think they should understand it, not complain about it), when people use the word *spiritual*, I don't think they have much idea at all of what they mean—except this: being spiritual means not being bound by the secular, naturalistic constraints of the Enlightenment. To be spiritual means that I believe there is something more, something beyond the reductionist "objective data" of modernity. All of reality isn't reducible to mathematics and physics plus nothing. "Just the facts, ma'am," is the creed of secular/scientific modernity. "Give me more than facts" is the plea of postmodernity—give me values, purpose, meaning, mission, passion, wisdom, faith, spirit. Early in the twentieth century, poet Edna St. Vincent Millay anticipated the impoverishment of a world reduced to "just the facts."

> Upon this age, that never speaks its mind
> This furtive age, this age endowed with power
> To wake the moon with footsteps, fit an oar
> Into the rowlocks of the wind, and find
> What swims before his prow, what swirls behind—
> Upon this gifted age, in its dark hour,
> Falls from the sky a meteoric shower
> Of facts . . . they lie unquestioned, uncombined.
> Wisdom enough to leech us of our ill
> Is daily spun; but there exists no loom
> To weave it into fabric.[2]

STRATEGY TWELVE C

In these powerful lines Millay captures the tragedy of Enlightenment-modernity: The era produced a shower of facts, but excluded the looms of imagination and faith needed to weave those facts into wisdom. Value-free and meaning-sanitized facts turned out to be valueless and meaningless to help us with our deepest ills. This is not to say that postmodern culture will be non-scientific or nonsecular; I would imagine it will be more and more so. But people will increasingly feel, when they look at secular institutions and scientific explanations, that "that's not all there is." Mystery will return, and with it, mysticism—and as a result, we Christians will have to remember and reclaim mystical approaches to faith we have largely forgotten for five hundred long years. (They are there in our history, but we have been so embarrassed about them during modernity that we hardly know they exist.)

This more mystical and spiritual focus will force us to change "lines of business" on the other side. During modernity we prospered in the Bible information business. We developed better, faster, and more enjoyable ways to deliver Bible knowledge (workbooks, study guides, conferences, radio shows) because knowledge was the great prize of modernity. What happens, though, when knowledge, information, and facts are as ubiquitous as advertising, with the result that their value decreases because supply exceeds demand? What happens when what people really want and need is not just Bible knowledge, but biblical spirituality? Do we know very much about helping people become not just more knowledgeable, but actually more spiritual? No doubt, a post-secular/scientific environment creates new opportunities for our churches, but do you see how it also creates new challenges? And can you see how we must "de-bug" our churches of their bias toward simply being transmitters of information if we are to be of spiritual service to people (and God) on the other side?

5. The Virus of Individualism

In the world of the personal computer and personal identification number, it's no wonder that Christianity was reduced to being a story about how to get a personal Savior—how to get my personal soul into heaven rather than hell. The virus of individualism was an autoimmune disease in the Body of Christ; it made parts of the body not recognize they were organically united to other parts. Instead of celebrating their connectedness, parts competed with, fought, rejected, and feared one another. In modernity it was me and Jesus, me and my Bible, me and my spiritual growth, me and my salvation. Even where the church came in, it was still all about me—getting my needs met, getting my soul fed, acquiring the religious goods and services needed for me and my happiness and my success.

Can we imagine an understanding of the gospel that's bigger than the salvation of my individual soul (as wonderful and miraculous as that is in itself)? Can we imagine an approach to the church experience in which "we" does not exist for "me"? Are we prepared for a time (this is coming, and now is) when our finely crafted me-oriented evangelism and our consumer spirituality of self-interest seem, not a step ahead and up to a better life, but rather a step down and backward into a narrow, cramped, more selfish life? Will we have the courage to let go of those approaches, to find better ones, new ones, ancient ones?

6. The Organizational Virus

When the virus of individualism hybridizes with the virus of mechanism, you get this new virus of organizationalism. Here individuals are little machines that function in the bigger machines of organizations. Can we imagine a form of Christianity that is in some way postorganizational? Can we figure out why, at the end of the modern era, "organized religion" feels like a bad thing, but "spiritual community" feels like a good thing?

7. The Consumerist Virus

During much of modernity, the medieval view of the church as societal institution endured. But as it increasingly lost its favored position, as secularism led other institutions (such as governments, media, the academy) to become increasingly hostile toward the church, the church in the late modern matrix morphed, evolved, and re-formed. In its Protestant, free-church forms, the church disappeared as an institution and reappeared as an enterprise: a "purveyor of religious goods and services," to borrow a damning and memorable phrase from Darrell L. Guder.[3]

If given a choice between seeing the church as an institution that must be preserved for its own sake, or seeing the church as an enterprise that exists to meet people's needs, I would definitely prefer the latter. But it is not hard to imagine how a consumerization of Christianity can lead to its bastardization. (If you have cable television, how different, really, is TBN from QVC?) Can we imagine a form of Christianity that has a different role in the world—neither societal institution nor purveyor of religious goods and services? How much would change if we could effectively filter out both institutional and consumerist viruses, and what new role would we find as a missional community?

THIS HURTS!

This kind of de-bugging, filtering, or scanning won't be easy or painless. What Dave Tomlinson says about evangelicals would, I think, hold equally true for mainline Protestants and Catholics:

> Is there a radical rethinking of the evangelical position in the light of cultural and academic developments? Or do we find the same old evangelicalism recycled and re-presented? I would suggest that it is nearer to the latter, and of course there are very many people who will say that this is precisely as it should be. Others would like to see a deeper review of traditional positions: a review which acknowledges more fully that the frame of reference in which evangelical tradition was formed has now changed drastically. The world at the close of the twentieth century is vastly different from that of the late nineteenth and early twentieth centuries, and this has far greater consequences than simply updating our approach and presentation of the gospel: it requires us to rethink the way in which the gospel is perceived.... it can only be done by facing the pain and uncertainty of a thoroughgoing rethink.[4]

Why is this process so painful? Imagine yourself a medieval Christian, a Roman Catholic monk, in 1520. Word is spreading about radical new ideas from some character named Luther in Germany. These ideas seem to challenge the authority of the pope and the church. How can Christianity stand without the authority of the church? If the foundational authority of the church goes, then all of Christianity will surely crumble with it. It is painful even to think about Christianity surviving the loss of what seems like its very foundation—painful and frightening.

Christians like you and me face a similarly painful thought process today. We can hardly imagine how Christianity could survive without the assumptions of modernity. But that is what we must do. Tomlinson continues,

> I have absolutely no doubt . . . there are significant numbers of people . . . who share a desire for the movement to undergo just such a radical rethink. I also know that those in positions of influence do not wish this to happen, and I understand why: they do not want anything to split the constituency. . . . My severe reservation about this strategy is that it holds the movement back from facing the challenges which it must confront.[5]

GUIDELINES FOR REVOLUTION

There is a word for this kind of rethinking and the change it will inevitably unleash. The word is *revolution*. How do we prepare for revolution? Let me, in closing, offer a few suggestions.

1. We must leave off all distractions and needless bickering. When big issues are at stake, one can't waste energy on small stuff. Many organizations are virtually paralyzed by their most conservative constituency, which keeps raising trivial or backward-looking issues. Ironically and unintentionally, these distractions threaten the very survival of these institutions because they distract them from the important work at hand—of reinventing, evolving, changing, creating, to stay "in the game" in this time of transition.

STRATEGY TWELVE C

2. We can't isolate. Individuals and groups must find broader communities in which open dialogue about the rethinking and revolution can take place. And those broader communities must include people who say things "we" have never thought about before.

3. We must make room for messy, creative thinkers. There is nothing easier than pouring cold water on new ideas or condemning Galileos. Creative thinkers won't have all the *i*'s dotted or *t*'s crossed; they bring us their tentative and unfinished rough drafts, not camera-ready copy. They can be testy, rude, and insensitive—not unlike an Amos or John the Baptist, unsettling us with prophetic insight. If we jump on their mistakes or incompletenesses, if we ignore their brilliance and focus on their gaffs, we will shut them down, scare them away, and squander our chance to learn from them ... just when we need them most. The proverb tells us that an empty stall stays clean, but that much work comes from the strength of an ox. Similarly, if we want the strength of creative thinkers in our barn, we will have to shovel some ... unpleasant stuff. But the benefits are worth the shoveling.

4. We must increase our commitment to God. At times when our ideas about God are being challenged, we have a unique temptation—and opportunity. The temptation? To become lax in our commitment to God. The opportunity? To prove that our faith is in God himself, in the God who may or may not match our conceptions, not just in our own beliefs about God, or in the God who always conforms to our preconceptions. There's a word for this reaching out in confidence and hope beyond our current understanding: faith.

5. We must keep doing what we know. In times of spiritual revolution we generally know less than we did six months ago or six years ago. This loosening up of our certainties can lead to a spiritual malaise or apathy, a dangerous carelessness, a loss of fervency of spirit. Whatever formulations we question, whatever assumptions we reconsider ... if

we stop loving God with all our heart, soul, mind, and strength, and if we stop loving our neighbors as ourselves, we will become casualties of the revolution. And revolutions do have casualties, so we must be careful.

6. We must be gracious. Of course, defenders of the status quo will see us as compromisers and threats to all they hold dear. Of course, good-hearted but less astute people will trivialize our concerns by singing a chorus of "Gimme that old time religion, gimme that old time religion . . . it was good enough for my father . . . it's good enough for me." Of course, kind but timid friends will advise us to moderate the revolution into a minor adjustment. And of course, some will not treat us with much kindness. We must choose in advance not to return unkindness for unkindness, but rather to be gracious . . . firmly pressing on, but gracious. Neither the abrasive nor the timid will inherit the earth, Jesus said, but the meek.

7. We must not be negative. It is easy to bash modernity. It is easy to bash the church. It is easy, and adolescent. What is hard, and what is more grown-up, is to move beyond critique and engage in creative formulation of new alternatives for the future. In transitions like this, as we have said, the "de"-work is important; it is necessary to identify our viruses and scan them out. But that kind of virus scanning can become addictive . . . and any computer person will tell you, when you're scanning for viruses, you're not getting anything new done. Perhaps in this decade, our work is 80 percent de-work, and 20 percent re-work. Maybe in the next decade it will be 50–50, and maybe in the following decade, 20–80. If we are in the year 2030 and we are still whining about modernity, somebody better tell us to shut up.

8. We must be hopeful. We must trust God. Jesus said he would build his church. If the gates of hell won't prevail against it, then certainly this historical transition isn't too big a threat. This thing is going to work out, with us or without us. None of us is indispensable, because the

church doesn't depend on any of us. Yet, if we are called by God to be agents of the revolution, then we must trust God for guidance (we'll need it!), mercy (we'll make mistakes), and protection (the dangers are many in times like this). And we must pledge our lives to the cause of the kingdom of God, which is always a revolutionary project anyway. As long as we are in that endeavor, we have reason for abounding hope.

9. We must not get distracted. At the end of the day, being a Christian isn't about being ancient, medieval, modern, or postmodern. It's about following Jesus, becoming more like him, participating in the kingdom he announced and invited us into, serving him. There is a place for this conversation about postmodernity; obviously, I believe that. But I look forward to the day when we can forget the term and focus as never before on the work of the kingdom of God.

10. We must keep learning—which will be our thirteenth and final strategy.

I recently received an email from a friend who is struggling with this revolution in his own faith. He said something like this: "When these kinds of thoughts have knocked at my door, I have always turned them away. I have always felt that if I let go of my rigid, rationalistic, modern approach to faith, with my perfect systematics and my bombproof formulations, I would fall away from God. So I have been afraid to 'go there,' afraid to admit I really had questions and even doubts about my modern version of Christianity. Now that I'm overcoming my fears and 'going there,' it's still not easy. This kind of thinking tears me up inside. But I must tell you, instead of falling away from God, I feel that I'm falling into God as never before."

"Falling into God"—not a bad place to be, I'm sure you'll agree.

Add to This List

*Help your church
become a learning
organization that discovers
and implements its own
new strategies.*

Our children, and their grandchildren, will inherit the new breed of churches and the new forms of Christian living we forge in the next twenty-five years. Because I love my children, I want to pass on to them a faith that's real—a good faith, a faith that is true and effective in launching them into fulfillment, mission, and community.

The twelve strategies we have considered so far will help us build churches with the flexibility and strength needed to thrive on the other side. But this thirteenth strategy is doubtless the most important of all because it suggests to us the need to keep learning. If our rate of learning doesn't keep up with the pace of change, our future is not bright. So it is not the application of these strategies that is most important, but rather our ability to keep learning and applying as yet unthought of strategies.

The fact is, we will never finish the transformation process we are considering. We will never get it all right and be able to relax in an eternal status quo—not in this life. It's like parenting: We get good at one phase, and our kids grow into another, providing us parents with the humbling experience of progressive incompetence. It's like building roads: They're never fixed or finished, but always in need of repair.

The church has taken many forms through history. The diversity of the physical architecture reflects deeper transformations, from cathedrals to country chapels, from catacombs to living rooms, from rented schools to leased storefronts, from converted barns and restaurants to a hut in the jungle or a clearing in the woods. The church on the other side will be at least as diverse as the churches of our history—but all at the same time. And the diversity will keep changing like the images in a kaleidoscope.

We cannot control the flow any more than we can control the wind, or the dinosaurs in Jurassic Park. Believing, as we do, that ultimately God reigns, we shouldn't really want to govern the church on the basis of our limited perspectives, should we?

AN ENDLESS SUPPLY OF STRATEGIES

So we must keep learning, surfacing new strategies to guide us in the Spirit, like sailors sensitively adjusting to the unpredictable movements of the wind over the waters. Many of these new strategies cannot be anticipated now; many can. For example, if I were writing a longer book, I might explore additional strategies such as the following.

1. Celebrate more.

Amid the changes we face, a lot is going right, and we need to strengthen all the good things that remain by celebrating them frequently. Churches that claim to have a faith that saves and a God who is truly good ought to be happy places. Joyful music, laughter, feasts, and general mirth and good cheer were desirable in other times of challenge and change (see Nehemiah 8:9–12, for example). I believe they constitute a strategy worth considering now. Christians have a reputation for furrowed brows, angry rhetoric, and wagging fingers. I would rather that we earn a reputation for joyful sanity and serenity, good clean fun, a quiet confidence in God that makes us smile at the future, and a childlike mirth for each new day that the Lord makes.

2. Be gentle.

A forgetfulness of the Lord's command to "judge not" has invaded our spiritual software, like a dangerous computer virus. We need better virus filters on the other side. How can we be prophetic without seeming pathetic in our critical fastidiousness? How can we learn to love more by believing the best more, to test all things and yet hold fast to what is good, to drain the bath water but keep the babies? The answer probably has to do in part with gentleness.

One of the worst things that could happen to you who read this book (and like it) would be to develop a critical and harsh attitude toward Christians who resist the other-side changes we have considered. (If I have displayed attitudes of this sort in these pages, I sincerely apologize.) These conservative brothers and sisters will only dig in their heels deeper if they are criticized, so our critique certainly won't help them. Instead, we need to be gentle.

After all, perhaps God isn't asking all churches to change. Perhaps God wants some churches to stay just as they are, maintaining a safe place for people who aren't wired for pioneering the church on the other side. Perhaps we would be cruel to wrench people from the music, preaching styles, liturgies, and thought patterns they love, and through which they sincerely revere God. Perhaps the real test of our gentleness will come when these very people become harshly critical of us for moving toward the other side. Perhaps being nonjudgmentally gentle is the most important element in this whole process.

3. Simplify, simplify.

Jesus had a way of streamlining faith to its grand essentials: Love God, love your neighbors. He assailed the Pharisees for creating spiritual loads too heavy for people to carry. In a world of hectic schedules, in which our modern laborsaving devices have only served to save us time for a still heavier workload, couldn't we use a shot of spiritual streamlining? Shouldn't the load be easier and the burden lighter if we are learning of Jesus on the other side?

4. Emphasize and de-emphasize place.

Inexpensive air travel, telecommunications, and the internet together serve to radically de-emphasize place, and this condition may have significant effects on the ways we do church. For example, on the other side, could a small group (composed of eight people on four continents) meet meaningfully in an on-line chat room for real-time fellowship and accountability? Will seminaries download information (text and video lectures), upload tests and papers, and interact via E-mail with students around the globe who never see a traditional classroom or library? If many locations are de-emphasized in these ways, will there be a corresponding reemphasis on the places where we actually do travel and assemble physically? Will there therefore be a resurgence in the importance of church architecture?

5. Enrich your gene pool.

On the other side, the local church (regardless of denominational status) may lose the luxury of being independent. Churches may need more than ever to get outside help from trusted consultants. Church boards may even have outside members—pastors of other churches, seminary professors, retired Christian workers, Christian lawyers and accountants and counselors and entrepreneurs—people whose expertise, distance, and outsider identity may bring a needed objectivity and breadth of insight. The "gene pool" of intelligence and experience possessed by a church's own members may be insufficient; the challenges we face may require us to ask for more help more often from more people.

FINAL QUESTIONS

Will you consider these strategies, rejecting what seems worthless and holding on to what is good? Will you think of other strategies I haven't dreamed of? Will we all be open to God doing a new thing in our lifetimes? Will we adjust our sails and take new tacks in the changing winds of the future? Will we seek humbly to teach and learn from one another? Will we offer help without pat answers and accept suggestions from one another without defensiveness? Will we be "dragged kicking and screaming" to the other side, or will we set out like intrepid pilgrims and sturdy pioneers? Will we keep learning, or will we act like know-it-alls?

I hope, by thinking these thoughts together, you and I will lead the way into the reinvented church, wisely, humbly, even joyfully, for the glory of God.

STRATEGY THIRTEEN

A PROMISE TO KEEP WITH YOU ──────────────────

I became a committed Christian during the Jesus Movement in the early seventies, a context in which being a Christian felt more like following a leader than accepting a code or creed. Granted, that joyful simplicity of faith was quickly complicated, and our spiritual innocence didn't last long. But even now, after all these years, I still think of being a Christian, not as a social or political thing, but as a Jesus thing. I see myself as one of those guys fortunate enough to have heard Jesus say, "Follow me."

Even now, I see myself—and you too—standing with the disciples on the shore of a lake. It is late afternoon, and Jesus tells us he will meet us later, on the other side after he has dismissed the crowd. And so we pile into a boat and begin our crossing. Then comes the storm. A hard wind seems to be against us. Night falls, and we grow fatigued and frightened. We feel caught in the middle: Do we press forward or turn back? A few of us are arguing for a return to the familiar shore. Then, in the middle of the night, in the middle of the lake, Jesus appears, and some pretty amazing things happen. . . . And eventually he climbs in the boat and we make it, tired and damp, but safe and sound to the other side.

Or I see us after the Resurrection. It is morning, and we have been fishing with our friends all night. We feel frustrated because we are succeeding at being neither fishers of men nor fishers of fish. Through the fog we see a man wave from the shore. He cups his hands to his mouth and yells, "Cast your net on the other side, boys!" And you know what happens next.

Or I see us some days later, this time in the mountains, and we have an ominous feeling that something big is about to happen. The risen Jesus appears and tells us what to do: Bring everyone we can into the new way of life he has taught us. And then he says, "Don't worry. I will be with you always—here, on the other side, and everywhere in between." That is a promise to hold dear.

Strategy Specifics

*T*his is a book of working strategies, not abstract speculations. Its greatest value will be realized as you
experiment with and implement those strategies that
ring true with the most relevance and urgency in your
situation. But how do you move from plans in your
head to action in your church? These exercises are
intended to help you extend your thinking toward practical application. There are several ways you can use
them.

1. You can do the exercises literally, which will get
   other people involved—those people who can
   then become a team or a catalytic force for
   change.
2. You can imagine doing these exercises.
3. You can adapt them for use in an ongoing small
   group, board, class, or team.
4. You can repackage them for use on a retreat or
   in a breakout session at a conference.

More exercises are provided than anyone would
probably be able or willing to do, so pick and choose
freely. Keep the goal in mind: They are designed to help
you translate ideas into action.

STRATEGY 1: *Maximize Discontinuity*

Get a group of pastors or lay leaders together to discuss
questions and topics like these:

1. Identify some small and incremental changes you have attempted in your church, and evaluate their effect.

2. Review the history of your church, and consider whether this Strategy's description of renewal fits your church's renewal experiences.

3. Discuss the possibilities of starting a new church that would be new in kind as well as age. What would it be like? Brainstorm, jotting down everything that comes to mind.

4. Would it be easier, in your opinion, to start a new church or to reconceive an existing one? Whom do you know that would be interested in such a venture? What costs and benefits can you list for each alternative?

4. Project what your church's future will be—five years, ten years, and twenty-five years from now—if it is not reconceived. At what point would reconception be most possible? (In other words, how desperate would your church need to be in order to consider more radical change?)

5. What things are nonnegotiables and unchangeables for your church, and why?

STRATEGY 2: *Redefine Your Mission*

In your small group, or in an upcoming leadership retreat, spend some time profiling what you think a "better Christian" looks like. Questions like these might stimulate your thinking.

1. If you grew up in a church, profile a "good Christian" as it was defined there. How has your profile changed since then? What remains the same? What is different? Why?

2. What must people know to be considered "good Christians" in your church or group? What must they do? Not do? Believe? Not believe? Get specific, because the devil is in the details.

3. If a totally untaught, irreligious person were converted and added to your church tonight, list the things that would have to happen for this person to be considered a good Christian, in terms of doctrine, behavior, and cultural patterns.

4. Do you ever worry that your group or organization has become pharisaical? What positive signs do you see that you are

more in tune with Jesus than with the Pharisees? What negative signs point the other way?

5. What are the unspoken mission statements active in your church or group? What difference would it make if your mission were redefined as this Strategy suggests?

6. Try boiling down your definition of a "better Christian" to a few irreducibles. Do it as individuals, and then go for a group consensus. Then come back in a few weeks and critique your profile.

7. Why does this question—defining what a good Christian is—seem so hard? What do you think Jesus would say about this discussion?

8. Imagine that 75 percent of the people in your country were Christians like those in your church. What would be the effect on the society at large? What about 35 percent? What about 10 percent? What about 100 percent?

STRATEGY 3: *Practice Systems Thinking*

Get a group of people together from a particular ministry within your church to talk about the church's program in general, and the program you work with in particular. Use questions like these to fuel your discussion:

1. If our church could be compared to a physical body, what would its essential systems be? (For comparison purposes, the essential systems of a human body include the muscular, digestive, skeletal, nervous, epithelial, lymphatic, reproductive, and circulatory systems.)

2. Which of those systems are strongest? Which are weakest?

3. Which needed systems may be nonfunctional or nonexistent in our church?

4. Categorize specific activities and meetings of your church in terms of various systems, such as outreach, teaching, spiritual development, assimilation, leadership and leadership development, management, and conflict resolution. Are some systems overprogrammed? Are some underprogrammed?

5. Think of examples of a program that worked very effectively for a while and then stopped working. Try to explain, in systems terms, the life cycle of that program.

6. Think of examples of programs that thrived in other churches and failed in yours, and vice versa. Why do you think this happened?

7. Discuss areas where you see in your program some of the systems observations at work, as described in this Strategy.

8. Can you think of times when your specific program interacted synergistically with another? Can you see recycling, symbiosis, or multiple function between one program and another? Can you see how your program has competed with another program?

9. How could programs be better coordinated in your church?

10. Do you see evidence of sick or dysfunctional systems in your church or ministry area?

STRATEGY 4: *Trade Up Your Traditions for Tradition*

1. Try to arrange a dinner party. Invite people from as many different Christian denominations as you can. Tell those you invite that it is going to be a party where we tell stories about growing up Baptist, Catholic, Methodist, Pentecostal, or whatever. Have no other agenda. Just tell stories. It should be a good time.

2. Investigate Richard Foster's Renovaré program. It is built on the premise that there have been five main streams in the Christian church at large and that whichever one you come from, you will be enriched and balanced by discovering the other four, by trading up your one tradition for the fivefold Tradition, one river that includes the contemplative, holiness, charismatic, social justice, and evangelical streams. (Renovaré, Inc., 8 Inverness Dr. East, Suite 102, Englewood CO 80112-5609. Phone: 303-792-0152.)

3. If this chapter is of special interest to you, I encourage you to follow it up by reading Robert Webber, *Ancient Future Faith* (Grand Rapids: Baker, 1999).

STRATEGY 5: *Resurrect Theology as Art and Science*

Go to a restaurant for breakfast with one or two friends. Over coffee (or the beverage of your choice), discuss questions like these:

APPENDIX

1. How has your theology changed in content in the last ten years? What specific doctrines or beliefs were you sure about ten years ago that you now question or have a different opinion about?

2. Why did these beliefs change, and what was the process of changing them?

3. What are the potential dangers associated with your changes of belief? What are the potential benefits?

4. If you were to boil down your theology to five to ten core beliefs, what would they be? Write them on a napkin or placemat there in the restaurant, if necessary.

5. Think of the most theologically astute person you know or have access to. Ask this person to join you for breakfast, and "assault" him or her (in a friendly way, of course) with honest questions. Let the restaurant be one place on earth where honest theological dialogue takes place.

6. End your breakfast with a humble prayer for guidance, illumination, and wherever necessary, forgiveness.

7. If your breakfast group wants to keep meeting to explore this subject further, I recommend Stanley J. Grenz and John R. Franke, *Beyond Foundationalism: Shaping Theology in a Postmodern Context* (Louisville: Westminster John Knox, 2000).

STRATEGY 6: *Design a New Apologetic*

Invite a group of non-Christian friends over for a party, and ask them one question. Then be quiet and listen. Let them teach you about apologetics. Any one of these questions should do:

1. Do you believe in God?

2. Why do you believe or disbelieve in God?

3. What do you like and dislike about Christians?

4. What do you like and dislike about non-Christians?

5. If you were looking for a church, what would you look for?

6. What could possibly ever make you want to look for a church?

7. Why should anyone believe in God?

8. What are the consequences of not believing in God?

9. What in your childhood religious background helped or hindered you in believing in God as you grew older?

STRATEGY 7: *Learn a New Rhetoric*

Here are a few activities to help you interact with the issues raised in this Strategy.

1. Get a group of people together and tell stories for an evening. Tell stories about times you felt close to God, times you felt abandoned by God, people who made God seem real, and people who tempted you to atheism. Tell stories that mix faith and humor, and faith and horror. At the end of the evening, have a time of prayer and tell God what you learned. Consider this evening an important preparation for communication on the other side.

2. If you are part of a Bible study or small group, invite a friend who is not a Christian to attend. It would be best if this were a rather confident, extroverted kind of non-Christian. He or she could be an atheist or agnostic, a Buddhist or a Muslim, as long as that person has had little or no exposure to Christian diction and concepts. Explain that you need his or her help. You want him or her to interrupt every time someone uses a term not understood, and the discussion cannot continue until that term has been explained to his or her satisfaction. At the end of this evening, discuss what you learned about the jargon of your faith community, and discuss the challenge of learning to translate so you can be understood on the other side.

3. Get a group of people together to critique a videotape or audiotape of a Christian speaker. Ask them to put themselves into the shoes of an "outsider"—someone unfamiliar with the speaker's Christian dialect. Stop the tape as often as necessary. Pay attention to illogical arguments, unconvincing methods of proof, confusing forms of illustration, unshared assumptions, and unwitting offenses. Of course, remind yourselves that you are not doing this exercise to be hard on the speaker, but to gain a better understanding of the issues raised in this Strategy. Remind yourselves to be gracious to others—but hard on yourself—so you can learn to speak in a way that will be understood on the other side.

APPENDIX

STRATEGY 8: *Abandon Structures as They Are Outgrown*

1. With a group of friends, make a list of five things you would like to change about the way your church works. Then imagine implementing those changes, and anticipate what the effects would be. Try to identify the progress and problems that would result. Then anticipate what changes would be recommended to deal with those problems.

2. Design a set of bylaws for a new church, with built-in "constitutional conventions" so that changes will be expected. See if you can anticipate what changes would need to be made at various critical milestones of size.

3. If you are able to field-test your ideas in a real-life setting, be sure to publish your results in a journal or newsletter so other churches can learn from your experience. Either that, or start a consulting business; your services should be in high demand on the other side!

4. Choose three insights from this Strategy that strike you as sensible and pertinent to your church. Discuss ways these insights could be implemented. Or, conversely, discuss why these insights are absolutely impracticable and hopelessly idealistic. After that discussion, consider them anyway, since the status quo is even more impracticable and unacceptable as we move closer to the other side.

STRATEGY 9: *Save the Leaders*

Get a group of laypeople together with your pastor or pastors. Include parachurch workers if you can. Spend a few hours listening to the answers to the questions below, but please observe this ground rule: No easy answers. Your job is to listen, to understand, to empathize, not to fix or correct. Honor your pastors by trying simply to understand them as fellow human beings—people like you who have devoted their careers, their lives, to a task that is extremely difficult in the best of times. Maybe, through your listening, your faith, and your prayers, you will help save them to do the impossible.

1. What makes ministry frustrating for you these days?

2. What double binds or "catch-22's" or impossible situations do you feel you have to live with?

3. What are the worst moments you recall in ministry, and what made them so terrible?

4. When have you been closest to quitting?

5. What will it take to save you as a leader?

6. If you could go back in time and speak to yourself when you were just entering ministry, what would you say, knowing what you now know?

7. Where, and with whom, do you feel safe? Who understands you, your work, and your challenges best?

STRATEGY *10: Subsume Missions in Mission*

1. Choose any three ideas from this Strategy that most interest or bother you. Find a friend to listen to your list, and then hear out his or her list.

2. Offer your pastor an interesting proposition: Develop a task force for revisioning your church as a missionary force to reach your community. Come up with as many ideas as you can, and then try to pick a few to put into practice in the next year. The fact is, on the other side, every location is a mission field, every church a mission agency, and every Christian a missionary. Your little task force can start acting the way it will (and should) be.

3. Write to your favorite mission agencies and cast your vote for innovation and change. Encourage them to read this Strategy. Remember that there are many donors in their constituency who will oppose all change, regarding it as a sign of decline and apostasy. Mission leaders are like trapeze artists who must let go of the trapeze they are grasping in order to reach for the new. Your letter of encouragement can help them during that moment of free-fall panic, assuring them that someone will be standing with them on the other side.

4. Imagine that you were given a million dollars to use for start-up of a sustainable mission initiative. Write up a "business plan" incorporating as many of the "bath-water-free project" characteristics as possible. Examples: A Mission to Reduce Racism and Promote Racial Reconciliation, A Mission to Involve Christians in

Environmental Activism, A Mission to Link Urban and Suburban Families in Redemptive Relationships, A Mission to Link Single Men with Fatherless Boys, A Mission to Start a New Congregation.

STRATEGY *11: Look Ahead, Farther Ahead*

1. Imagine that Christ won't return for a thousand more years. Consider what the church might look like in the year 3000 A.D.

2. Someone out there: Write a science fiction novel (or at least a novella) set in the twenty-fifth century, in a context in which the Christian faith is alive and well. Help us to envision that possibility.

3. If you are a pastor, plan, in about a year or two, to preach a series of sermons on eschatology. In the meantime, try to pry up the nails of traditional paradigms and try to see the Scriptures afresh, especially the teachings of Jesus. Read them in light of the fact that God must have intended them to be valid, not just for a generation or two, but for this whole span of time. Try to capture their spirit, their attitude, their posture, their view of history. See what happens as those sermons develop.

4. If you are a church member, try to quell division and horror as your pastor preaches the above series of sermons.

5. If you are a seminary or college professor, ask your students to research life in Europe in 1000 A.D. Then ask them to imaginatively put themselves in the position of a medieval priest trying to envision the world at the dawn of the third millennium. See if this exercise unleashes creative thinking about our future.

STRATEGY *12A: Enter the Postmodern World—*
Part A: Understand It

See if you can find a few friends who would represent postmodern, modern, and traditional viewpoints as described in this Strategy. Have them read the Strategy and then talk about these questions.

1. Which are you—traditional, modern, or postmodern—and what do you like about your cultural paradigm? Do you feel like an amphibian, a cross between two or even all three? In what ways?

2. Postmodernism may be too unstable to be a long-term worldview. It may be a transitional phenomenon between the modern age and something as yet unseen. What would you predict to be a post-postmodern worldview, or would you argue for a long reign for the postmodern paradigm?

3. If you have read much of the generational literature distinguishing boomers from busters (etc., etc.), could it be that the underlying differences between generations have less to do with one's birthdate than with one's posture in relation to the emergence of postmodernism? For example, might the boomers who bravely enlisted to fight in Vietnam and later became the Reagan-revolutionary yuppies of the '80s have been the more modern-minded boomers? And might the boomers who were the hippies of the '60s and '70s—and who have stayed more or less counter-cultural since—be the more postmodern-minded boomers? And might those who were liberal hippies in the '70s and then more conservative yuppies in the '80s simply be "bilingual," able to metamorphose like amphibians from postmodern to modern and so on, whichever is more advantageous at the moment? And might busters be the first generation for whom postmodernism is the majority view?

4. Consider some other examples from popular culture: perhaps the *Star Trek* series (togetherness in space, the prime directive of noninterfering tolerance), *Seinfeld* reruns (togetherness in an apartment), or *The X-Files* (the truth is out there, but you should trust no one; there is more out there than meets the modern eye). What connections can you see with thoughts presented in this Strategy?

5. It has been said that love means entering someone's world without judgment. Do you feel you can enter postmodernism with more understanding than judgment, and why?

APPENDIX

STRATEGY 12B: *Enter the Postmodern World—*
Part B: *Engage It*

See if you can coax a few Christian friends to get through these two long and difficult Strategies with you so you can discuss them together. Encourage them to write notes in the margins so you can share your annotations. Then try a few of these questions:

1. There is much to disagree with in these Strategies. I may have overstated my case for effect. In your opinion, what are my most obvious overstatements? Are there any tiny grains of truth mixed in with the chaff? Do you think anything is understated?

2. Church leaders are going to face huge problems in the next twenty or thirty years if postmodernism turns out to be as important as these Strategies claim. At first, most of the new converts will be postmoderns while most of the established Christians will be moderns.

   a. What problems can you foresee if this is the case?
   b. How can these problems be minimized or averted?
   c. What lessons can we draw from the Jew-Gentile controversies in the book of Acts and the Epistles?
   d. Eventually some church leaders will be postmoderns. What strengths and weaknesses might they bring to the table?
   e. Who are the best candidates to be the first postmodern leaders in your church, and how can they be welcomed in, integrated with, and protected?

3. Sara Toth suggests a special problem for Christian leaders whose congregations contain those who "just don't get it" as far as postmodernism goes:

> We need to learn to handle ambiguities, paradox, we need to embrace the fear of not knowing, in humble dependence upon the One who alone knows. My problem is: how can this be communicated to the average church member? In many cases the options of the sensitive thinker in a teaching position is [sic] that he will either keep his ambiguities to himself and preach/write differently, and ultimately lose his

faith; or he will say what he thinks, thereby risking discrimination and being labeled skeptic, agnostic, etc.[1]

What would you do if you were in this situation? Can you think of any other options?

4. Choose three of the listed "opportunity maximizers" that you feel most positive about. Why do you feel that way? How could your church implement these maximizers?

5. We are talking about a truly radical change here. Do you favor the direct or indirect approach to dealing with it? Do you think that postmodernism will be a divisive issue, that there will be modern and postmodern churches much as there have been charismatic and non-charismatic or liberal and evangelical? How can these twentieth-century contrasts instruct us to deal better with postmodernism in the twenty-first century? What position should your church take?

6. Whether or not you agreed with these two Strategies, did you have fun with them? Do you feel a sense of accomplishment in simply having followed them through to the end? Did you think some new thoughts? Do you see both danger and opportunity?

If you could bring a group of people together to discuss this chapter, you could ask everyone to rate his or her response to this chapter on a scale of 0 to 10, with 0 signaling near-total disagreement and discomfort, and 10 signaling enthusiastic endorsement.

After giving everyone an opportunity to express the "why" behind one's responses, do something daring. Divide the group in half, with the most enthusiastic in one group and the least so in another. Then ask groups to "switch sides." In other words, ask those most resistant to this chapter to take on the role of its supporters, and vice versa. Engage in some lively debate about specific points in the chapter, such as the seven viruses of modernity or the ten guidelines for navigating the revolution. After a good hour or more of dialogue, drop your roles and offer some final feelings and thoughts about the exercise and the chapter.

APPENDIX

STRATEGY 13: *Add to This List*

1. Find some Christian teenagers. They probably won't want to read this book (maybe I'm wrong), so you summarize it for them. Then ask them for their ideas for the church on the other side. Try to get them dreaming.

2. What's right with your church? What strengths can you celebrate? How can you avoid a judgmental spirit and remain gentle as you move toward the other side?

3. The most obvious aspects of change in churches these days—casual dress, more contemporary music, the use of drama, the importance of small groups—are hardly mentioned here. Why do you think they have not been emphasized? How do these changes relate to the thirteen Strategies in this book?

4. Which of the five additional Strategies mentioned in this Strategy resonate best with you? Why?

5. What are you going to do about this book? How will it affect you? Who else should read it?

6. What items would you like to add to this list of Strategies? (I would be honored to see your ideas in writing. You can write me at 2410 Spencerville Road, Spencerville, MD 20868.)

NOTES

INTRODUCTION

1. Lyle Schaller, *It's a Different World* (Nashville: Abingdon, 1987), 20, 237.
2. Ken Blanchard, *Forum Files* 4, no. 3 (Tyler, Tex.: Leadership Network).
3. Francis Schaeffer, *The Church at the End of the Twentieth Century* (Downers Grove, Ill.: InterVarsity Press, 1970), 81–82.

STRATEGY ONE: MAXIMIZE DISCONTINUITY

1. Margaret Wheatley, *Leadership and the New Science* (San Francisco: Berrett-Koehler, 1992), 3–4.
2. William Easum, *Sacred Cows Make Gourmet Burgers* (Nashville: Abingdon, 1995), 16–17, 19, 21–22.
3. *NetFax*, no. 11 (23 January 1995); published by Leadership Network, Tyler, Tex. Phone: 800-621-8268.

STRATEGY TWO: REDEFINE YOUR MISSION

1. Charles Colson, "Wanted: Christians Who Love," *Christianity Today* (2 October 1995), 112.
2. C. S. Lewis, *God in the Dock* (Grand Rapids: Eerdmans, 1994), 70.

STRATEGY THREE: PRACTICE SYSTEMS THINKING

1. Peter Senge, *The Fifth Discipline: Mastering the Five Practices of the Learning Organization* (New York: Doubleday, 1990), 68–69.
2. See, for example, *Prepare Your Church for the Future* (Grand Rapids: Revell, 1991).

STRATEGY FOUR: TRADE UP YOUR TRADITIONS FOR TRADITION

1. Sally Morgenthaler, *Worship Evangelism: Inviting Unbelievers into the Presence of God* (Grand Rapids: Zondervan, 1995), 132, 134.
2. See his book *The Transforming Friendship* (Batavia, Ill.: Lion Publishing, 1989).
3. Beginning with *The Celebration of Discipline* (San Francisco: Harper & Row, 1978).
4. Robert Webber, *Signs of Wonder* (Nashville: Abbott Martyn, 1992), 87–88: quoted in Morgenthaler, *Worship Evangelism*, 135.
5. See also Robert Webber's *Ancient-Future Faith* (Grand Rapids, Baker, 1999).

STRATEGY SIX: DESIGN A NEW APOLOGETIC

1. See C. S. Lewis's argument on the evolution of mind in *Miracles* (New York: Macmillan, 1946).
2. Pope John Paul II, *Crossing the Threshold of Hope* (New York: Random House, 1994), 80–81. See especially the pope's discussion of *semina Verbi* in "Why So Many Religions?"
3. George Hunter, *How to Reach Secular People* (Nashville: Abingdon, 1992).

STRATEGY SEVEN: LEARN A NEW RHETORIC

1. Dietrich Bonhoeffer, *Letters and Papers from Prison* (New York: Macmillan, 1971), 299–300.
2. Walker Percy, *The Message in the Bottle* (New York: Farrar, Straus, and Giroux, 1954), 116, 118.
3. Romano Guardini, *The Lord* (Washington, D.C.: Regnery Gateway, 1954), 73.
4. Ibid., 148.

STRATEGY EIGHT: ABANDON STRUCTURES AS THEY ARE OUTGROWN

1. Larry E. Greiner, "Evolution and Revolution as Organizations Grow," *Harvard Business Review* 50 (July 1972): 37–46.
2. Quoted in William Easum, *Sacred Cows Make Gourmet Burgers* (Nashville: Abingdon, 1995), 105.
3. This insight, by the way, takes a huge stride forward beyond transition-zone talk about wine and wineskins, substance and structures. The general assumption in the transition zone is that someone actually has the new wineskins—packaged and marketable through their book or seminar or consultation—and that these new wineskins would be ever-new, never becoming brittle or restricting. In the new world it is assumed that today's new wineskins will be tomorrow's old ones, and so on.
4. Easum, *Sacred Cows Make Gourmet Burgers*, 29.

5. Ed Simon: quoted in Peter Senge, *The Fifth Discipline: The Art and Practice of the Learning Organization* (Garden City, N.Y.: Doubleday, 1994), 343.

STRATEGY NINE: SAVE THE LEADERS

1. Robert Bly, *Iron John* (New York: Vintage Books, 1992), ix–x.
2. "An Interview with George Hunter," in *Next* 2, no. 2, p. 3: in reference to *Church for the Unchurched* (Nashville: Abingdon, 1996). For a superb treatment of team leadership, see George Cladis, *Leading the Team-Based Church* (San Fransisco: Jossey-Bass, 1999).
3. David Fisher, *The 21st Century Pastor* (Grand Rapids: Zondervan, 1996), 7–9.
4. Archibald Hart, *Coping with Depression in the Ministry and Other Helping Professions* (Dallas: Word, 1984), 12.
5. William Easum, *Sacred Cows Make Gourmet Burgers* (Nashville: Abingdon, 1995), 141–42.
6. Bill Hybels, *Rediscovering Church* (Grand Rapids: Zondervan, 1995), 17.
7. Henri Nouwen, *Name of Jesus: Reflections on Christian Leadership* (New York: Crossroad, 1993), 29–30.
8. Hybels, *Rediscovering Church*, 193.
9. For an outstanding exploration of leadership during transitional times, see Alan Roxburgh and Mike Regele, *Crossing the Bridge: Church Leadership in a Time of Change* (Costa Mesa, Calif.: Percept Group, 2000).

STRATEGY TEN: SUBSUME MISSIONS IN MISSION

1. James F. Engel, *A Clouded Future?* (Milwaukee: Christian Stewardship Association, 1996), 134. See also James F. Engel and William A. Dyrness, *Changing the Mind of Missions* (Downers Grove, Ill.: InterVarsity Press 2000).
2. Lesslie Newbigin, *The Open Secret* (Grand Rapids: Eerdmans, 1995), 144–45.
3. See, for example, Mike Johnson, "Mission Financial Practices and Church Growth in Yugoslavia," a paper for Mission Forum (July 1988), P.O. Box 150, 8100 Bratislava 1, Slovakia. E-mail: miro@sen.ext.eunet.sk.
4. Paul McKaughan, "Missions in the 21st Century," unpublished report of the Evangelical Foreign Missions Association (January 1995).
5. Sadly, in both religious and secular circles, it has become common to refer to the "amazing stretching numbers" of people or money found in missionary reports as "evangelastic." For example, "the crowd numbered about five hundred, evangelastically speaking."
6. See Eddie Gibbs, *In Name Only: Tackling the Problem of Nominal Christianity* (Wheaton, Ill.: Victor, 1994).
7. Thomas Wolf, *Intent* (Fall 1995): 3; P.O. Box 35, Cascade, CO 80809-0035.

8. McKaughan, "Missions in the 21st Century."

9. Bob Buford, *Halftime: Making Sure Your Best Years Are Ahead of You* (Grand Rapids: Zondervan, 1995).

10. See, for example, Engel, *A Clouded Future?*

11. William Easum, *Sacred Cows Make Gourmet Burgers* (Nashville: Abingdon, 1995), 8.

12. Mike Regele, *Death of the Church* (Grand Rapids: Zondervan, 1995), 220.

STRATEGY ELEVEN: LOOK AHEAD, FARTHER AHEAD

1. Carl George, *Prepare Your Church for the Future* (Grand Rapids: Revell, 1992), 19–20.

2. Philip Yancey, *The Jesus I Never Knew* (Grand Rapids: Zondervan, 1995), 80.

STRATEGY TWELVE A: ENTER THE POSTMODERN WORLD—PART A: UNDERSTAND IT

1. Bob Fryling, *Being Faithful in This Generation: The Gospel and Student Culture at the End of the 20th Century* (Downers Grove, Ill. InterVarsity Press, 1995).

2. Three notable exceptions are J. Richard Middleton and Brian J. Walsh, *Truth Is Stranger Than It Used to Be: Biblical Faith in a Postmodern Age* (Downers Grove, IL: InterVarsity Press, 1995); Stanly Grenz, *A Primer in Postmodernism* (Grand Rapids: Eerdmans, 1996); and Leonard Sweet, *Soul Tsunami* (Grand Rapids: Zondervan, 1999).

3. Michael Crichton, *The Lost World* (New York: Ballantine, 1995), 391.

4. Ibid., 393.

5. Rinus Baljeu: quoted in *Intersect* (Fall 1996); 1763 Slaterville Road, Ithaca, NY 14850.

6. D. A. Carson, *The Gagging of God: Christianity Confronts Pluralism* (Grand Rapids: Zondervan, 1996), 13ff.

7. See 1 Corinthians 9 in Eugene H. Peterson, *The Message* (Colorado Springs: NavPress, 1993), 415–16.

8. The newsletter *Intersect* consistently carries articles that show this understanding: 1763 Slaterville Road, Ithaca, NY 14850. Phone: 607-277-3333. Fax: 607-272-2389. E-mail: ct25@juno.com.

9. Reprinted in *Perspective* (4 November 1996), from Richard Halverson, *Somewhere Inside of Eternity* (Portland, Ore.: Multnomah Press, 1978), 50.

STRATEGY TWELVE B: ENTER THE POSTMODERN WORLD—PART B: ENGAGE IT

1. D. A. Carson, *The Gagging of God: Christianity Confronts Pluralism* (Grand Rapids: Zondervan, 1996), 10.

2. *NetFax* no. 43 (15 April 1996); published by Leadership Network, Tyler Tex. Phone: 800-621-8268.

3. "Understanding Nothing," from the album *Big Circumstance*, 1989, Gold Castle Records.

4. Mark 4:24.

5. Mike Regele, *Death of the Church* (Grand Rapids: Zondervan, 1995), 216.

6. Lesslie Newbigin, *Proper Confidence: Faith, Doubt, and Certainty in Christian Discipleship* (Grand Rapids: Eerdmans, 1995).

7. Matthew 26:38; 27:46.

8. Dennis Haack, "The Glory of God and Human Culture: How Do We Influence Postmodern Society?" Gospel and Society Conference, Bratislava, Slovakia (June 1996), 7.

9. Watchman Nee, *What Shall This Man Do?* (Fort Washington, PA: Christian Literature Crusade, 1979): quoted in Richard Foster and James Bryan Smith, eds., *Devotional Classics* (San Francisco: Harper Collins, 1993), 342.

10. Consider, for example, turning water into choice wine (John 2), confronting the woman at the well (John 4), asking unusual questions (as at the pool called Bethesda, John 5), and walking on the water (John 6).

11. Lesslie Newbigin, *The Gospel in a Pluralist Society* (Grand Rapids: Eerdmans, 1996), 22.

12. Nancey Murphy, *Beyond Liberalism and Fundamentalism: How Modern and Postmodern Philosophy Set the Theological Agenda* (Valley Forge, Pa.: Trinity Press, 1996), x.

STRATEGY TWELVE C: ENTER THE POSTMODERN WORLD—PART C: GET READY FOR REVOLUTION

1. John Caputo and Michael Scanlon, *God, the Gift, and Postmodernism* (Bloomington: Indiana University Press, 1999), 1–2.

2. Edna St. Vincent Millay, "Huntsman, What Quarry?" (1939).

3. Darrell L. Guder, ed., *The Missional Church: The People of God Sent on a Mission* (Grand Rapids: Eerdmans, 199?).

4. Dave Tomlinson, *The Post-Evangelical* (Nashville: Abingdon Press, 1995), 25–27.

5. Ibid., 26.

APPENDIX: STRATEGY SPECIFICS

1. Sara Toth, "Being Church in the Post Modern Age," Gospel and Society Conference, Bratislava, Slovakia (June 1996), 4.

ABOUT THE AUTHOR

*B*rian McLaren graduated from the University of Maryland with degrees in English (B.A. and M.A., summa cum laude). After teaching in higher education for several years, he left academia to become founding pastor of Cedar Ridge Community Church, an innovative church near Washington, D.C. (www.crcc.org). He serves on several boards and is a well-known speaker with special interest in evangelism, apologetics, church growth, art and music, and pastoral survival and burnout issues. He is active in the Terranova Project, an initiative within Leadership Network, and helps coordinate the Theological Working Group (www.terranovaproject.org). His interests include wildlife, ecology, fishing, hiking, music, and travel. He is married to Grace, a consultant in team-building and related issues. They have four teenagers, one of whom is a cancer survivor. His *Finding Faith* (1999) is also available from Zondervan.

MORE READY THAN YOU REALIZE

Evangelism as Dance in the Postmodern Matrix

BRIAN D. MCLAREN

WARNING: This is not just another book on evangelism. This book contains fresh, encouraging, challenging, groundbreaking, and doable ideas you'll want to share with your pastor, your small group or class, your board, or your parachurch organization.

This book draws on the author's experiences and in a striking way. The context for this book is a series of real email conversations between McLaren and a cyberseeker. McLaren uses these conversations to elicit insights into the changing nature of evangelism in these postmodern times. And in fact, he shows why the most profound synonym for the word evangelism is the term disciple making.

OUT: Evangelism as sales pitch, as conquest, as warfare, as ultimatum, as threat, as proof, as argument, as entertainment, as show, as monologue, as something you have to do.

IN: Disciple-making as conversation, as friendship, as influence, as invitation, as companionship, as challenge, as opportunity, as conversation, as dance, as something you get to do.

You're more ready for this than you realize, and so are your friends!

Softcover 0-310-23964-8
www.crcc.org
www.emergentvillage.org

Pick up a copy today at your favorite bookstore!

ZONDERVAN™

GRAND RAPIDS, MICHIGAN 49530 USA

WWW.ZONDERVAN.COM

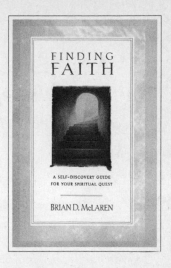

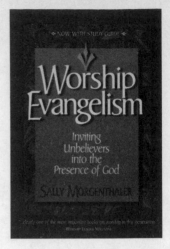

We want to hear from you. Please send your comments about this book to us in care of zreview@zondervan.com. Thank you.

ZONDERVAN™

GRAND RAPIDS, MICHIGAN 49530 USA

WWW.ZONDERVAN.COM